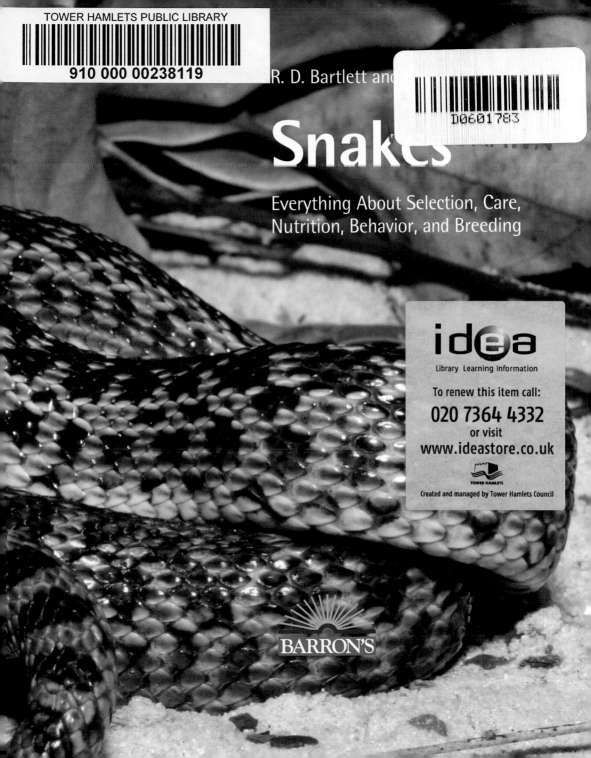

R. D. Bartlett and

# Snakes

Everything About Selection, Care,
Nutrition, Behavior, and Breeding

**BARRON'S**

# CONTENTS

# CAPTIVE CARE

*Once a hobbyist decides to acquire a snake, the question then becomes: What kind would be best? The choices offered by even a small pet store can be overwhelming.*

## Choosing a Snake

When deciding on a snake, numerous questions need to be asked, involving how much room you have for the terrarium, what you feel most comfortable feeding the snake, whether you can maintain a constant tropical temperature or whether a variable temperature is more usual in your house, and whether you want a captive-bred or a wild-collected specimen? Why these questions?

Well, if you only have space for a 10-gallon (37.8 L) terrarium, you wouldn't buy a snake whose adult size exeeds a two-foot (61 cm) length. If you want to feed your snake worms or fish, neither a rat snake nor a kingsnake would be the correct choice. If your winter indoor temperatures vary nearly as much as the outdoor temperatures, you should not consider a tropical emerald tree boa.

As regards the final question, it is less likely that a captive-bred and born or hatched snake will harbor as many endoparasites as a wild-

*Rough green snakes are one of the few insectivorous snake species commonly kept captive.*

collected specimen, but a captive-bred one *may* be a little more costly.

After reading this book, you may decide that a garter, brown, or rough green snake would all be good choices for a 10-gallon (38 L) tank. None are large; all eat worms, fish, or insects: all are from temperate climates and can withstand a reasonable degree of temperature fluctuation (including a period of winter hibernation, should you choose to provide it): and none are particularly costly—whether wild-collected or captive-reproduced.

However, if you have always dreamed of having a big snake, and local regulations permit this, have lots of room to devote to caging, don't mind feeding your snake rabbits and can afford to do so, and can provide a rather constant year-round temperature, a big boa or python might be perfect for you. These are also discussed herein.

The time to make all of the decisions pertinent to snake keeping is *before* and not after your purchase. The proper decision will save you much unnecessary agonizing and ensure that you and your snake have an enjoyable, lengthy relationship.

## Caging and Keeping Suggestions

Most pet snake species are undemanding animals. They require feeding perhaps once a week; some can fast for months without any deleterious effects. Fresh water (see restrictions for aridland snake species on page 45) and adequately sized cages are easily supplied.

When deciding on caging, do not be deceived by a snake's common name. For example, although the members of the natricine genus *Nerodia* are called water snakes, they spend the better portion of their days (and all of their nights) on tree limbs, out of the water. Captives, when kept in an aquarium setup or even in an overly damp terrestrial terrarium where they cannot dry off, will develop skin lesions, which can be fatal.

Because of the availability of commercial reptile cages, it is unnecessary to convert aquaria into terraria, though you can.

The responsible snake owner will provide captive snakes the most naturalistic surroundings possible. We don't delude ourselves that we can recreate nature, but we do try hard to make the snakes feel safe, secure, and at home, and cage furnishings figure prominently.

**Cage furniture:** This term describes virtually any and all cage decorations, whether a simple wooden snag, an inverted cardboard hidebox, growing plant, or a plastic vine.

For climbing surfaces or limbs, most snakes seek the stability of firmly affixed, sizable limbs. The slender and almost feather-light rough green snake can be found in twig tips, but even it prefers the stability offered by vine tangles. Provide limbs one and a half times the diameter of your snake's body. Either wedge the limbs firmly in place or glue exact lengths into place, using aquarium sealant.

## Venom

Snakes of many genera—hog-nosed snakes, garter snakes, and others—possess a Duvernoy's gland. This gland, located anterior to the enlarged teeth of the upper jaw, is associated with venom production. Not all snakes with a Duvernoy's gland are considered venomous. However, in some cases, when humans have been bitten by these "harmless" snakes, reactions consistent with mild envenomation have occurred.

In reality, we know very little about the possible venomous properties of Duvernoy's glands. Toxic results have occurred from snakes as common as the backyard American garter snake of the genus *Thamnophis*. Human fatalities have actually resulted from bites by the Asian genus *Rhabdophis*. Some researchers even classify the tiny and innocuous ring-necked snakes of the genus *Diadophis* as a venomous species. In fact, new findings have led such noted researchers as Dr. Sherman Minton to pose the question, "Is there such a thing as a nonvenomous snake?" The answer is probably yes, but those with Duvernoy's glands should be considered at least mildly venomous.

Some snakes, like the hog-nosed and tentacled snakes, are reluctant to bite, even when wild. Other species, such as American garter and water snakes, may bite with even gentle handling. Always use extreme care when handling any snake. A bite can cause several bacterial infections. Wash any bite thoroughly with soap and water.

We also place heavy logs on the terrarium bottom. The snakes may rest on or behind them. Place the logs directly on the cage bottom (not atop the substrate) or secure them so that a burrowing snake can't be crushed under them.

Secretive by nature, most snakes spend their time in hiding, some more persistently than others, especially during daylight hours. Captive snakes use a hide box or other place of concealment. If forced to stay in the open, many will become stressed and refuse to eat, especially if their cage is in a heavily trafficked area and if it is one of the more nervous species.

A readily replaceable small cardboard box with an access hole cut in one side will suffice. Pet stores often have preformed plastic "caves" and combination cave/water dishes that are washable, sterilizable, and last for years. We have used natural hollow limbs and hollowed cactus skeletons that are readily found in woods and fields. These can be used as floor furnishings or can be Silastic-secured at suitable levels in the terraria. Corkbark is a reasonable alternative to the hollow limbs and is much lighter, more impervious to body wastes, easily cleaned and sterilized, and available at many pet stores, reptile dealers, and plant nurseries. A hide box is important when the snake is getting ready to shed and its eyes turn "blue." It is then more secretive than usual.

## Lighting, Heating, and a Comment on Weather Patterns

**Staying warm:** Snakes are ectothermic, using outside sources of heating and cooling to regulate their body temperatures. They warm themselves by basking in a secluded place.

Although tropical and semitropical snake species may remain active all year round, northern snakes hibernate. Snakes in regions that are subject to periodic cold spells may become dormant only during those cold spells.

Although semiactive, these snakes may not feed for most of the cooler time of the year.

**Staying cool:** It is as important for snakes to remain as comfortably cool as warm. During hot weather or where temperatures are naturally very hot, most snakes become nocturnal or aestivate (undergo a period of warm-weather dormancy) through the weeks of excessive heat. Desert snakes may be diurnal during cool weather and nocturnal during the hot summers.

Thermoregulation is important even for captive snakes. They, of course, are dependent on us, their keepers, to provide them with caging that lets them select their optimum body temperature. Warming the cage may be done using heating pads or heating tapes placed under a portion of the cage flooring. (Hot rocks are not recommended.) Ceramic heating units that

*Darkened areas of seclusion (hides) should be provided for all snakes. Many styles are commerically available and others are easily made.*

screw into a light socket and light bulbs (especially those with directed beams such as flood and spotlights) are other possible sources of heat, and the bulbs provide light. Maintain a "hot spot" temperature of 80–87°F (27–31°C). Fluorescent bulbs provide little heat, which can be advantageous in warmer areas where additional heat is not needed.

Night temperatures should be cooler by several degrees than daytime temperatures (from 75–85°F [24–29°C]).

**Light:** Natural light cycles are nearly as important as temperature. Under normal conditions, snake activity is greatest during the longest days of the year (which just happen to coincide with the most optimum temperatures as well). Snakes that hibernate will do so during the shortest (and coldest) days of the year.

═══════════ T I P ═══════════

### Heat Sources

Heating sources include incandescent bulbs, ceramic heating "coils," heating pads, and heating tapes. To provide a heating gradient, these are best situated in one end of the terrarium.

**Full-spectrum/ultraviolet light:** When asked whether ultraviolet illumination is necessary for snakes, our answer typically is that while it may not be absolutely mandatory, it sure can't hurt. Water snakes seem to benefit from full-spectrum UV lighting, especially for basking and for their skin condition. We provide full-spectrum lighting above each cage and use color-corrected plant-growth bulbs for heating. The color temperature of full-spectrum bulbs—a way to measure the amount of natural sunlight-like light—may be beneficial to captive snakes and is undoubtedly beneficial to insectivorous species.

**Weather and behavior:** Naturally changing weather patterns, such as dry seasons, rainy seasons, low-pressure frontal systems, the high pressure associated with fine weather, even the lunar cycle, are known to affect snake behavior. Many nocturnal snakes are most active during the dark of the moon or during unsettled weather. Tropical snakes may be most active at the start of the rainy season

*Besides incandescent bulbs and heating pads (both shown), many additional choices of cage heaters are readily available.*

or just before or just after nighttime downpours. Reproductive behavior is often stimulated by the elevated humidity and lowering barometric pressures at the advent of a storm.

**Water, soaking bowls, and cage humidity:** Although the many aridland (desert and savanna) snake species may drink and soak less often than the more humidity-tolerant woodland species, water is important to all.

Maintaining the correct humidity can be an important consideration in the successful maintenance of snakes. Species from humid areas will have shedding problems if the humidity is too low; species from desert areas can develop serious (even fatal) health problems if the humidity is too high. In this latter case, aridland species, such as Trans-Pecos and Baja California rat snakes, may languish if kept in the perpetual high humidity of our southeastern coastal plain states. Many successful breeders of these species suggest providing water to them only one or two days a week.

Besides serving as a drinking receptacle, the water bowl is an integral part in raising or lowering the humidity in a cage. Cage humidity will be higher in a cage with limited ventilation than in one with more. To increase and retain a high humidity in your cage, place a large water bowl near, not on or under, the hottest spot. To decrease or keep humidity as low as possible, provide a small water dish and place it in the coolest spot in the cage.

To make certain you're not depriving your animal of water, watch its behavior. Snakes often prowl actively when thirsty.

# Caging

## Simple "American Style"

American reptile enthusiasts usually select the bare minimum in caging; absorbent substrate of folded newspaper, paper towels, or aspen shavings; "untippable" water bowl; and hide box. Many snake species will thrive, and some (such as corn snakes and many milk snakes) will even breed in such cages.

Plastic shoe, sweater, and blanket boxes, commonly used, are available in many hardware and department stores. The lid must fit securely or be secured with tape or Velcro strips. Aquariums used as terrariums are somewhat more expensive but also readily available in pet and department stores. Locking plastic or metal-framed screen lids are standard items.

For plastic boxes, sufficient air (ventilation) holes must be drilled (or melted) to provide air transfer and to prevent an accumulation of humidity. Ventilate at least two sides, if not all four. For an aridland rat snake, ventilate the top as well.

Cabinets that hold a dozen or more plastic boxes are now available, many with built-in heat tapes. These are advertised in reptile magazines and available at reptile shows.

Glass aquaria can be oriented in either the horizontal or vertical position. The clip-on screen top can serve as a side for vertical orientation. Glue feet on the tank's underside so the side or top is easy to take off and put on.

Custom glass terraria can be purchased or, if you are handy, built. Take your measurements, cut the pieces of glass (or have them cut), burnish the edges, then use a latex aquarium sealant. The glass can be held in place with strips of masking tape while the sealant is curing (about 24 hours). When using the latex, make certain that the edges of the glass that are to be sealed are entirely free of oils or other contaminant that could prevent the sealant from forming a tight seal. Remarkably large terraria can be held together very securely with aquarium sealant, especially if the tanks will not be used to hold water.

## European Style

Unlike the plain terraria of American hobbyists, Europeans are known for more elaborate, natural terrarium interiors. Their concept of creating a miniaturized ecosystem has allowed them to breed species thought difficult by Americans. Their approach is to match the terrarium setting to the species.

*Depicted here is a very simple and suitable cage for small, slow moving snake species. Of course, a tightly fitting cover is mandatory.*

You will have to decide which concept you prefer. It is much easier to care for large numbers of specimens in rather sterile, generic cages than in intricate terraria.

We use a combination of both concepts, using a substrate of easily replaced dried leaves for a woodland terraria or sand for a desert terraria. The water dishes are hidden behind logs gathered from the woodlands. Whenever possible, we have at least one thicket of easily grown foliage plants. Philodendron and Epipremnum (=Pothos) have proven very durable in moderate light situations. Diagonal and elevated limbs are placed strategically for arboreal snakes.

Moisture content in naturalistic and semi-naturalistic terraria must be evaluated frequently. If these terraria are too damp, too dry, or have incorrect lighting, the vegetation and snake inhabitants will both suffer.

*Smaller snakes (tri-colored kingsnakes are shown) may be kept in properly ventilated plastic shoe or sweater boxes.*

*Shelving units of many styles are commercially available for storage.*

*Commercially available cages are available for snakes of all sizes.*

# Feeding

Snakes exhibit all degrees of dietary generalization and specialization. Many feed on birds and mammals, and it is these that are often favored by Americans. For a captive snake to eat properly, it must be offered the correct type of food and feel secure or it will not feed, regardless of how hungry it may be.

## Mechanics

Snakes find their prey by sight and scent. They can apparently see moving objects well (whether snakes perceive stationary objects is questionable). In addition to sight, snakes have an acute sense of smell. For example, scent molecules are carried by the tongue of the rat snake to the sensory Jacobson's organs nestled in the palate, where they are analyzed.

Snakes may overpower their prey by means of constriction, by throwing a loop of their body over and partially immobilizing a large prey item, or by eating the prey while still alive.

Constriction does not result in broken bones or other damage to the prey. Rather, as the prey exhales, the constricting coils of the snake tighten. Inhalation soon becomes impossible, and the prey suffocates. Once the snake determines the prey ready to be eaten, positioning and swallowing begins. The snake may entirely release its hold on the prey, or, while retain-

*Tightly covered vertical aquaria will allow arboreal snakes to climb.*

ing its hold, sidle its jaws to the head (or, more rarely, the feet) to begin the swallowing process.

Nearly everything about a snake, beginning with the jaw structure, is "elastic." All tooth-bearing bones, upper and lower, are capable of independent movement. Designed to retain a hold, the conical teeth are all recurved. To swallow prey, it (usually) extends and then retracts the upper and lower jaw bones on one side and then the other side. In this manner, it almost glides (or walks) around its prey. Inside the throat, contractions of the neck push the prey into the stomach. According to ambi-

ent temperature and its metabolism, digestion may be slow or rapid. During this time, the snake is quieter than usual, oftentimes moving no farther than necessary to effectively thermoregulate.

Contrary to conventional wisdom, snakes neither feed entirely on live food nor do some even prefer it. We have seen snakes in the wild find and eat dead rodents. We feed our captive snakes thawed, once-frozen mice and rats.

**Seasonal appetites:** A snake's appetite often wanes with the approach of the shorter days of winter, especially if it is from a temperate area and more so if it is wild caught.

If your snake is a temperate species and a winter nonfeeder, you can either accept the situation and cool the animal into a state of dormancy (see hibernation on page 29) or you can fuss with the snake, changing its lighting, warmth, and feeding parameters, and hope that you can induce feeding before the advent of spring automatically does so. Letting nature take its course with cooling is easier.

Many stop feeding during breeding season. This fasting involves both sexes and is especially seen among boas and pythons. Females may fast for several days or weeks prior to egg or clutch deposition.

If your snake stops eating (but it isn't a gravid female, isn't time to hibernate or cool, and isn't breeding season), do the following:
• ascertain that the hiding areas are still accessible;
• increase the cage temperature by 3–7 degrees;
• increase the cage humidity;
• increase the daylight lighting intensity (the use of full-spectrum lighting may help offset the effects of the lessened hours of daylight).

If these methods fail, even when used in combination, try to enhance the acceptability of the prey items offered. Gory though it may seem, exposing the brain of a pre-killed food item will often induce eating again.

If a new snake doesn't want to feed:
• try all of the above suggestions;
• try varying prey species, size, and color (some might readily eat a half-grown brown gerbil but refuse one of another size, or a *white* gerbil of *any* size, or any color mouse);
• present the food *very* quietly, laying it nose first in the doorway of the snake's hidebox.
• move slowly and quietly.

## Diets

Earthworms are an excellent food item for many species and subspecies of garter snakes and brown snakes. In many areas of the eastern and Pacific United States, nightcrawlers and worms emerge from their burrows after dark on dewy or rainy nights and may be collected. They can be purchased from bait stores or bait suppliers (see ads in outdoors magazines for sources), or raised in the cellar or garage if temperatures permit. A bed of rich, porous loam will be necessary for the worms. Although we have never been able to produce enough for our needs, raising worms does allow us to purchase fewer from bait stores.

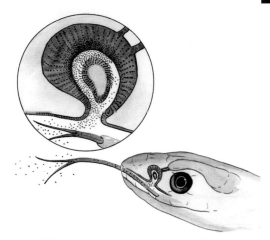

*A snake's tongue brings scent particles into contact with the sensory Jacobson's organ where the scents are analyzed (enlarged cross-section above).*

Live feeder fish can be purchased from tropical fish stores, bait stores, or collected if laws and time allow. Many snakes will also eat frozen (and thawed) food fish (such as smelts) or even fish fillets, but these are less nourishing than live fish and often have a higher fat content. We suggest these be used only occasionally to augment the primary diet of live fish.

**Frogs, goldfish and bait minnows:** Although goldfish are often used extensively by the keepers of fish-eating reptiles, many farm-bred fish contain an enzyme detrimental to reptile health. Goldfish should be used **only** as an emergency food source, if at all.

Frogs are a main food item of cribos, king, garter, and water snakes. There is no easy way to raise frogs for food. If necessary to feed these to captive snakes, feeder frogs can be purchased in dozen or larger lots from many reptile and amphibian dealers, or, where legal, they may be collected from the wild. Because

## Prey Size

Although most are capable of eating prey larger than their body diameter, if stressed (by fear, thirst, or temperature extremes) a snake is more apt to regurgitate a larger meal. As a rule, we never feed items larger than its body diameter.

most frogs harbor endoparasites that may be transferred to the snakes, avoid using frogs as a food item when possible. If you do feed frogs, the snakes to which they are fed should be periodically monitored for endoparasites and treated for them if necessary.

*Most snakes have multiple rows of recurved teeth.*

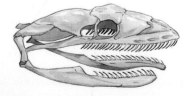

*Although wild, this young rat snake resided in the shrubs surrounding our home and would accept prekilled mice from forceps.*

Many frog species are now protected by law. As amphibian populations continue to decline, other species will likely also be protected. Some species (pickerel frogs and many tree frogs) contain noxious chemicals. If you provide frogs as a food, use only non-noxious and unprotected forms.

Toads are the primary natural dietary item of both the eastern and southern hog-nosed snakes. All cautions regarding using frogs as a food source equally apply to toads. The introduced giant toad, *Bufo marinus*, is known to produce *very* virulent toxins.

**Mice and rats:** Commercial breeders of mice, rats, rabbits, and chickens are a good source of feeder animals—live or frozen (we recommend the latter because they will keep almost indefinitely in your freezer). They may be purchased at many pet stores and reptile dealers, or you may raise them.

**Breeding mice and rats:** Mice and rats are easily bred. A single male to three or four females in a 10- (mice) to 20- (rats) gallon (38–76 L) tank (or rodent breeding cage) produces a steady supply of mice for your snakes. Every six months, let some of the young grow up to replace the adult breeders and feed off the old breeders.

Aspen or pine shavings can be used as bedding for your rodents. Feed mice a "lab-chow" diet specifically formulated for them or a healthy mixture of seeds and vegetables.

Fresh water must always be present.

**DO NOT** use cedar bedding. The phenols in cedar can harm reptiles or amphibians.

Some snakes refuse lab mice or accept them reluctantly. You may need to provide some species of wild mice (we use white-footed mice, *Peromyscus leucopus*, purchased from specialist breeders or collected from the wild.).

**Live versus dead mice:** We feed once-frozen, fully thawed and warmed mice to our snakes. In a cage, a live rodent (or baby chick) can become the aggressor. If, for some reason, you think you *must* feed live rodents to your snakes, never leave the cage unmonitored while the live rodent is present.

One way to thaw frozen feeder rodents is beneath the bulbs or on the lighting reflectors on the snake cages. You can also place them in a jar of hot water. It is *very* important that they are *thoroughly* thawed before being eaten. Do *not* thaw in a microwave because the thawing is not only uneven (creating pockets of intense heat while leaving other spots still frozen), but it further weakens an already weakened body wall, often making the rodent unusable. Present the rodents to the snakes, nose first, in long hemostats. Most are eagerly accepted.

**The (possible) benefits of a varied diet:** Growing evidence suggests that what is natural for a snake in the wild is the best diet in captivity. Although in the wild many snakes feed on one type of prey, other types eat almost anything they find or kill. Humans tend to offer whatever is easily obtained, usually lab mice or rats. As a result, we try to adapt toad-eating hog-nosed snakes to a diet of mice, and we feed cribos only rats. Not enough is known about the overall effects of a mouse diet on hog-nosed snakes. Could a more natural diet make indigo snakes, considered difficult to breed, more easily bred in captivity?

*Captive-bred Mexican-lined gopher snakes,* **Pituophis lineaticollis,** *are now readily available to hobbyists worldwide.*

**Scenting:** Scenting one prey type with the odor of another is a way to get *some* difficult-to-feed snakes to eat. This can be done in several ways. We know a specialist breeder of all three species of hog-nosed snakes who soaks mice intended as food for eastern and southern hog-nosed snakes in water in which toads have been frozen. When a hatchling rat snake is reluctant to accept a pinky, we rub the snout of the pre-killed mouse against a live green or squirrel tree frog or touch the mouse's nose to

## Mice Versus Toads for Hog-Nosed Snakes

See above and page 100 for a discussion on the controversial practice of acclimating the toad-eating eastern and southern hog-nosed snakes to a diet of mice.

some uric acid from an anole's stool and reoffer the pinky. It is seldom refused.

There are times when a snake will simply
refuse to feed and force-feeding may be necessary, but even this does not always correct the
problem. Neonates that won't eat may be fed
with a "pinky pump," loaded with a pre-killed
newly born mouse and inserted into the mouth
of the snake. This breaks down the body wall of
the mouse and forces the pinky into the throat
of the snake; from there it is usually swallowed.
Larger snakes may need larger meals. Even with
careful force-feeding, some snakes still fail to
thrive. Consult your veterinarian.

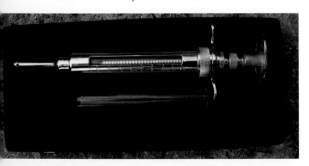

*Force-feeding a snake is traumatic for the
animal. "Pinky pumps" have been developed
to ease the force-feeding experience.*

# Health

The chances of successfully keeping a snake
of any species in captivity over a long period
of time are better if you start with a healthy
snake. However, determining the health of a
potential acquistion may be difficult to do.
Snakes, like all reptiles, may show no outward
signs of ill health until they are seriously ill.

Observing a snake's basic behavior is one of
the best ways to assess its condition. Select a
snake that displays an alert demeanor but is
not overly aggressive when disturbed. Some
species are more belligerent than others and
may have to be handled with a hook. Corn
snakes are fairly calm, whereas a speckled
kingsnake can be very defensive. Boas and
pythons *normally* act very differently than
kingsnakes, and a cribo or a racer is entirely
unlike a rat snake in *normal* responses. Large
snakes must be supported when lifted.

In addition to looking for a calm snake,
choose one of the hardier species. Again,
knowing that a rubber boa is a *much* more difficult species to keep than one of the closely
allied rosy boas will help you make a decision.

Select a snake that has good body weight.
Although some species are normally more slender than others, a length-wise skinfold along
the sides or "accordion" ribs is a caution sign.
If possible, watch the snake feed.

A sneeze may indicate a respiratory infec-
tion; labored breathing may suggest lung
flukes. Both are hard to diagnose in a living
snake. A postmortem diagnosis is frustrating
for you and pointless for the snake.

Until you know what is normal for the snake
in which you are interested, it is important to
read up on the species. This book should help,
and there are several monthly publications that

## Caution

Wild mice carry diseases that can be transmitted to humans. Don't handle them as casually as you might lab mice.

focus on snake behavior and husbandry. Seek the advice of someone knowledgeable; determining what is truly normal for a given species or subspecies will take hands-on experience.

With good care, snakes can become responsive and live for a long time. Many species live more than 10 years in captivity and some even live to 20 or 30 years. If you choose carefully, you can become a satisfied hobbyist.

## Shedding—What Is Normal?

The health and age of your snake will influence the frequency with which it sheds its skin. A healthy, fast-growing baby will shed its skin several times a year, much more frequently than a slowly growing adult or an ill specimen. A snake with a skin disease such as blister disease will shed frequently in an effort to rid itself of the diseased skin. If the skin problem is corrected, all evidence of the disease will often disappear after two or three sheds. Conversely, if conditions are not corrected, the problem may get worse and result in death.

The shedding process (also called molting, or, more properly, ecdysis) results from thyroid activity. A week prior to shedding, as a new skin forms under the old, your snake's pattern will dull to an overall grayish or silvery sheen. Its eyes will temporarily look bluish. A snake in

*Cloudy eyes and hazy coloring are an intergral part of the skin-shedding cycle of all snakes.*

# TIP

## Our Tip

Examine the shed skin to ensure that the eyecaps have been shed. Sometimes the old skin may adhere to the tailtip or the eyes. If not manually (and very carefully) removed by the keeper, the dried skin can restrict circulation, resulting in the loss of the tailtip or, if on the eyes, impaired vision and eventual blindness.

this phase is colloquially referred to as "blue" or "opaque" by hobbyists. The eyes will clear again, and after about a week, the snake will rub its nose against a log or rough spot to loosen the old skin at the lips. Once the skin is loosened, the snake will simply crawl out of its old skin and again be as brightly hued and patterned as before.

It is important that no patches of old skin remain attached. If it seems to have difficulty

*If manually restraining a snake becomes necessary, it should be accomplished slowly and gently. A Russian rat snake is shown.*

shedding, place it in a damp cloth bag overnight (make sure to check the temperatures). This will usually loosen the old skin and allow your snake to shed. You may have to occasionally help your snake rid itself of a particularly resistant shed.

In the wild snakes seldom have problems shedding, but captives may due to the stress of a new import, dehydration, starvation, or low relative humidity in the cage.

# ━━━ T I P ━━━

## Handling

Gentle handling will quiet many snake species. A snake hook is indispensable for a short-tempered snake. Gently restrain the head if it is in hand. For a large snake, support the body in several places. Never place a large snake on your shoulders or around your neck.

## Quarantine

When you bring your new snake home, quarantine it for a few weeks or even a month to avoid introducing diseases and parasites to other snakes. During quarantine, observe your new snake frequently, watching for labored breathing, sneezing, or continual loose stools. Have a fecal specimen examined by a qualified reptile veterinarian before you place the new specimen with others.

The quarantine area should be completely removed from the area in which other reptiles are kept—preferably in another room. Wash your hands between handling your quarantined and long-term specimens.

**Why bother?** This quarantine period is important. During this period of isolation you will be able to notice most health problems, whether established or incipient. Feeding schedules can be established, and your specimen can become at least semiaccustomed to the presence of people near its quarters. The importance of quarantine can do a great deal toward preventing later health problems.

## Ectoparasites

Snakes from the wild as well as captive specimens may harbor mites and ticks.

**Ticks** are readily seen and removed. Coat it first with Vaseline. (Use a cotton swab if you don't want to use your fingers.) After a few minutes, its grip will loosen, and you can use tweezers to grasp it by its head and gently pull it out. Check that the mouthparts are removed intact, and crush it before disposal.

**Mites** are more difficult to combat because they are smaller and often present in immense numbers, which can debilitate the snake due to blood loss. We once used a pervasive insecticide called "No Pest" strip. Cut into one-inch (25 cm) squares and placed atop the screen cover of a cage, the airborne insecticide killed mites. We always removed the water dish during the five-day treatments. An alternate treatment is injectable Ivermectin (administered by your veterinarian) or a dilute Ivermectin spray that you can mist onto your snake.

## Burns, Bites, and Abscesses

Prevention of these problems requires just a little forethought on the part of the keeper.

**Burns:** Incandescent lightbulbs and fixtures should be kept in a part of the cage that your snake cannot reach or covered with a snake-proof wire cage. Make sure the surface of your hot rocks or blocks does not go above 95°F (35°C). If your snake sustains burns, cool the burned area and apply a clean, dry dressing until you can get it to your veterinarian.

**Bites:** Snakes may be bitten by cagemates (usually when multiple males are housed together during the breeding season) or by feed animals. Rats being constricted may bite; a rodent left unattended in a snake's cage might chew on its predator.

Only use pre-killed prey for your snake. If you don't want to do the killing yourself, you can purchase frozen rodents.

**Abscesses:** An improperly sterilized and healed burn or bite may result in an abscess.

*Snake mites are not always easily seen. If your snake moves in a jerky manner, has puffy skin surrounding the eyes, or spends an inordinate amount of time in its water bowl, check it carefully for mites. A gentle misting with dilute Ivermectin is an effective mite treatment. A rough-scaled python is shown.*

*Although seldom present, ticks are usually easily visible and may be manually removed. A Trans-Pecos rat snake is shown.*

Some will heal and slough off or be rubbed off; a few may require surgical removal. Consult your reptile veterinarian.

## Respiratory Ailments

**Why it's serious:** Because snakes have only one working lung, unchecked respiratory problems can become quickly fatal. The cause may be bacterial, viral, or even a parasite. A medi-

cation that works effectively for one species of snake might not work as well for another species. Some aminoglycoside drugs ideally suited for curing a given respiratory problem may be so nephrotoxic that they can kill the snake if it is slightly dehydrated. Some bacteria are resistant to traditional antibiotics, such as ampicillin, amoxicillin, tetracycline, and penicillin. We suggest that you seek veterinary assessment of any respiratory problem. You can help by quarantining the sick snake in a separate cage and by elevating the cage temperature (and sometimes by reducing the relative humidity).

## Infectious Stomatitis (Mouth Rot)

**Diagnosis:** Uncorrected mouth rot is an insidious and common disease that can result in permanent disfigurement and even death. Stress, mouth injuries, and unsanitary caging conditions contribute to this disease. It is characterized by areas of white, cheesy-looking exudate along the snake's gums, enough to force the lips apart. Use cotton swabs to remove the exudate. Then wash the affected areas with hydrogen peroxide. Sulfa drugs (sulfamethazine is the drug of choice) are

effective against the bacteria that cause this disease. A veterinarian may suggest an antibiotic as well. Complete eradication of mouth rot may take up to two weeks of daily treatment.

## Blister Disease

**Diagnosis:** If your snake develops tiny raised spots or nodules (these may be hard but are often pus-filled) on its skin, immediately assess its caging. Excessively high humidity, damp and dirty substrate, and soaking in an unclean water dish cause this. Certain kingsnakes and water snakes seem especially susceptible. Blister disease can be fatal.

To alleviate the problem, start by cleaning and sterilizing the cage. Change the substrate, put in a smaller water bowl, and remove any plants. If the blister disease is minimal, your snake will probably enter a "rapid shed cycle" and rid itself of the problem within a shed or two. If it is advanced with underlying tissue damage, it will be necessary to rupture each blister and clean the area daily for 7–14 days with dilute Betadine and hydrogen peroxide. Your snake will enter a rapid shed cycle, and after two sheds its skin should appear normal.

## Medical Treatments for Endoparasites

Many reptiles, even those that are captive bred and hatched, may harbor internal parasites. When the snake becomes stressed due to

*"Star-gazing" is one manifestation of inclusion-body disease. At the moment, this problem seems restricted to boas and pythons and can be spread by mites. Initially, the disease is difficult to diagnose and a cure is not yet known.*

poor husbandry or another illness, the parasite load may grow to an untenable level. Because of the difficulties in identifying endoparasites and the necessity to administer dosages based on body weight, eradication of internal parasites should be handled by a qualified reptile veterinarian. Here are a few of the recommended medications and dosages.

**Amoebas and trichomonads: Metronidazole** 40–50 mg/kg orally. The treatment is repeated in two weeks.

**Dimetridazole** can also be used, but the dosage is 40–50 mg/kg administered daily for five days. The treatment is then repeated in two weeks. All treatments with both medications are administered once daily.

**Coccidia:** Many treatments are available.

The oral dosages of **sulfadiazine, sulfamerazine,** and **sulfamethazine** are identical. Administer 75 mg/kg the first day, then follow up for the next five days with 45 mg/kg.

**Sulfadimethoxine** is also effective. The initial dosage is 90 mg/kg orally, to be followed on the next five days with 45 mg/kg orally. All dosages are administered once daily.

**Trimethoprim–sulfamethoxazole** may also be used. The dosage is 30 mg/kg administered once daily for seven days.

**Cestodes (tapeworms):** Several effective treatments are available.

## Medical Abbreviations Identified

**mg** = milligrams (1 mg = 0.001 gram)
**kg** = killigrams (1,000 grams; 2.2 pounds)
**µg** = microgram (1 µg = 0.000001 gram)
**IM** = intramuscularly
**IP** = intraperitoneally
**PO** = orally (per os)

**Bunamidine** may be administered orally at a dosage of 50 mg/kg. A second treatment occurs in two weeks.

**Niclosamide**, orally, at a dosage of 150 mg/kg, is also effective. A second treatment is given in two weeks.

**Praziquantel** may be administered either orally or intramuscularly. The dosage is 5–8 mg/kg and is repeated in two weeks.

**Trematodes (Flukes): Praziquantel** at 8 mg/kg may be administered either orally or intramuscularly. Repeat treatment in two weeks.

**Nematodes (roundworms):** Several effective treatments are available.

**Levamisole**, an injectable intraperitoneal treatment, should be administered at a dosage of 10 mg/kg. Repeat treatment in two weeks.

**Ivermectin**, injected intramuscularly in a dosage of 200 µg/kg is effective. The treatment is repeated in two weeks. Ivermectin can be toxic to certain species.

**Thiabendazole** and **Fenbendazole** have similar dosages. Both are administered orally at 50–100 mg/kg and repeated in 14 days.

**Mebendazole** is administered orally at a dosage of 20–25 mg/kg and repeated in 14 days.

# Obtaining Your Snakes

The hobby of keeping reptiles is, of course, not limited to any one region of the U.S., Europe, or Asia. However, the commercial availability of reptiles is better in some regions than in others. In the U.S., for example, the major reptile dealers are in California, Florida, and New York. Reptiles are usually air-freighted to pet shops, hobbyists, or breeders.

We believe that breeders are one of the best sources of parasite-free, well-acclimated specimens and information about them. Most keep records of genetics, lineage, fecundity, health, and any quirks of the reptiles. Their records are usually available to customers.

Reptile swap meets or "expos" are another excellent source. One of the largest is a two-day annual event in Daytona, Florida. About 400 breeders and dealers gather to offer the public thousands of captive-bred reptiles. At any reptile expo, we advise that you know both the product you seek *and* the vendor who sells it, personally or by reputation.

## Conservation

Conservation is no longer "for the other guy." In today's world, it should be a concern of everyone, especially those who love nature and her creatures. Despite frequently heard arguments, it is our belief that the cause of reptile conservation is not any better now than before the keeping and breeding of snakes became a mainstream hobby. With their increased popularity, there may be proportionately more snakes collected from the wild now than 25 years ago.

All indications are that many snakes, even those once thought abundant, are being seen in the wild with less frequency. We don't yet know all of the environmental pressures causing population declines, but the declines seem real. We do know that collecting from the wild for the pet and leather trades, coupled with ever-increasing traffic casualties and ever-fewer remaining suitable habitats, are putting pressures on native reptile populations. Each additional specimen taken out of habitat becomes proportionately more important.

We urge you to explore the joys of field study and photography as opposed to field collection of snakes. If your budget allows,

consider a photography trip to the Amazon or elsewhere with a reptile-oriented eco-touring company. We have taken several such trips with Margarita Tours of Miami, Florida. On each trip we have had the opportunity to see and photograph more than 75 species of reptiles and amphibians. There is no equal to seeing snakes in their forest and desert habitats.

If collecting snakes is your goal, however, we ask that you purchase captive-bred and born specimens even if they are somewhat more expensive than wild-collected specimens.

## Getting Them Yourself

Many hobbyists would like to collect from the wild a few of the snakes which interest them. Keep in mind that many states within the United States, most South American countries, and several European countries have strict conservation policies which require specific permits for collecting or keeping native species. We urge you to check and abide by all existing laws, both for your own area and for the area you plan to visit.

In the U.S., federal laws often intermesh with or supercede state laws. Request information from the Department of the Interior. Penalties for breach of the laws (which can apply not only to collecting, but to transportation and sale or purchase of various species as well) can be severe. Find an up-to-date listing online. Also, see John Levell's *A Field Guide to Reptiles and the Law*. Laws are an always-changing process, and Levell's book includes the addresses of all pertinent protection agencies.

After checking the laws, research the life history of the snake you hope to find. Many are nocturnal, so be prepared to search at night. Familiarize yourself with all lookalike dangerous species, and be careful.

## The Name Game

As you advance in this hobby, you will definitely notice that the same snake may be called by different common names and sometimes by different scientific names. Sometimes this is honest dealer error but usually (with the common names at least) it is a part of what we call the "the name game." We find it as aggravating as you undoubtedly will. How can the name of the same species vary? And, while we're at it, of what possible good are those hard-to-pronounce Latin names?

Let's take the last first. Scientific names provide a degree of uniformity. The scientific names are always the same and are readily recognized by herpetologists and advanced herpetoculturists throughout the world.

The art of creating or selecting a scientific name for plants and animals is called taxonomy. The method that we currently use can be credited to the 18th-century Swedish botanist Carl (Carolus) Linnaeus (von Linne). Linnaeus' first compilation of names appeared in 1735 in a publication entitled *Systema Naturae*. His method is referred to as the Linnaean system of binomial nomenclature.

It essentially means that everything gets two names, much like our own two names.

The names used are based on Greek or Latin origins. For instance, a garter snake is *Thamnophis sirtalis*. *Thamnophis* is the genus (plural: genera), the equivalent of your surname. A genus consists of a group of species having similar structural characteristics. The genus is always capitalized and, if repeated is usually abbreviated to the first letter (still capitalized) followed by a period.

The term *sirtalis* designates the species, a group of similar organisms that are able to interbreed and produce viable offspring. The species name is not capitalized.

Scientific names are always differentiated from surrounding text by underscoring or italicizing. Scientific names don't change—or if they do change, they change far less than common names.

Common names may vary geographically or by whim. If a snake doesn't sell well under one common name this week, a canny dealer just might change its name on next week's list. Last week's "green-lined snake" could well be next week's "emerald thread snake."

If in your field work it is necessary to roll logs or otherwise disturb the environment, alter the area as little as possible. Carefully replace all rocks, logs, fronds, or other cover after moving them. Use restraint; take only the number of specimens you need.

Transport your catch quickly and safely. Protect it from excesses of heat or cold at all times. Small snakes may be transported in covered plastic deli cups. Larger specimens may be transported in tightly tied cloth bags.

If the collected specimens are a humidity-loving type, place a dampened, crumpled paper towel in the cup or bag with them. If desert dwellers, the paper towel should be dry.

In all cases, get the snakes to their permanent cages as quickly as possible.

In the ideal world, you could just hop on a bus or a plane and visit the reptile dealers in New York, Miami, or Los Angeles. You'd be able to go in the back rooms to see the really good stock that perhaps has just come in or is still under quarantine. You could point to this snake or to that snake and select those you wish to examine, purchase, and take home with you.

We're long past the days when the only way to get a snake was to go and pick it up. Now, when you've done your research and you know the snake you want, but it isn't a native species to your area and you're going to have to go through a dealer in another state—all you have to do is send an email or pick up the telephone. The bigger dealers rely on out-of-area sales for their livelihood, and shipping out-of-state is not a big deal for them. You can order from an out-of-area dealer or specialty breeder and be very happy with the result.

**Dealers**

In the United States, the largest reptile dealers are located in California, Florida, and New York—cities where there are international airports and customs offices. The reptile dealers sell (and ship) to other dealers in other cities who, in turn, supply pet shops, reptile breeding businesses, and individuals. Pet shops pay the wholesale rate; individuals pay the retail rate. There is usually some overlap among these businesses.

The continuing growth in popularity of reptiles has created specialty breeders/dealers. Specialty dealers usually breed reptiles themselves and deal directly with other breeders worldwide; they are often better able to answer your questions about the animals they breed. The animals on their lists have been acclimated, well fed, and have often been subjected to a veterinary checkup. It is from the specialty dealers that the broadcast selection of a genre, such as rat snakes, is usually available.

Locate the dealer who has the kind of snake you wish to purchase. Go online, or call and ask for a copy of their latest list of species available for sale. If you see a listing for a species you're interested in and it reads "Russian Rat Snakes, *Elaphe schrencki*, CB 14", 3.3" the dealer has three males ("3.") and three females (".3"). Generally speaking, the dealer will set the price and add the shipping expenses (usually about $65

*Many snake importers are located in California, New York, and Florida.*

*Open and inspect your purchases as soon as possible after they arrive. Contact your supplier immediately if a problem exists.*

per shipped box), and that's what you'll end up paying. The dealer may charge you for the styrofoam shipping box as well—it's wise to ask if there is a charge for boxing.

Once you both agree on the snake—the sex, age, color morph (if any), and price—you'll give your charge card number to the dealer. You'll be invoiced when the snake is shipped to you.

As part of the pricing negotiations, you'll give the dealer your name, your shipping address, and a daytime contact phone number. Dealers usually ship one or two days a week, timed to avoid weekend closed times at some carriers.

By the time you and the seller finish your conversation, you'll know what day your animal will be shipped and what day to expect it. The door-to-door shipping services now available mean good things for your new snake and for you—the snake will only be in transit for one day (two at the very most), and you'll know when your snake will arrive.

If there's a problem: Unless otherwise specified, reliable shippers guarantee live delivery; however, if there is a problem, you'll have to file a report with the shipping company and report the problem to the shipper.

After the first time, you will find that having an animal shipped to you isn't much of a problem. Understanding the system will open wide new doors of acquisition.

# REPRODUCTION

*Often the first reaction you will have when you show your friends your new pet snakes will be: "Are you going to breed them?"*

In the early years of snake-keeping, getting snakes to breed indicated that you had "the touch"—to make snakes behave as in the wild. People who got live babies from a breeding pair were highly regarded. Now it is not extraordinary. Businesses such as *The Gourmet Rodent* produce and wholesale thousands of baby colubrid snakes a year. For those who breed snakes on a much less formal basis, informally tagged "backyard breeders," breeding snakes is a way to make money, or at least make them pay for their own upkeep.

If you have a sexual pair of nonvenomous snakes, there's no reason you shouldn't breed them as long as a few caveats are covered before you begin—or rather before you set things up so the *snakes* can begin.

**1.** What will you do with the baby snakes? Before you produce any young, have willing buyers/friends lined up. For a species that has a dozen or so eggs, that may be all you need. But some snakes will surprise you with a large

*After an incubation of nearly two months, an amelanistic corn snake greets the world.*

clutch—red rat snakes can lay as many as 30 eggs. Are you coldhearted enough to freeze those "excess" eggs? And is that how you want to deal with the problem?

Don't assume your local pet store will buy your young snakes or even take them for free. Chain pet stores have centralized procurement systems for all their supplies, including livestock ("livestock" in the pet world means exactly that: live stock) and the manager cannot take live stock from a nonvendor.

**2.** If you live in a municipality, city coding officers may take a dim view of your breeding operation. They may regard it as a commercial enterprise, and if you aren't zoned for that (and residential areas are residential, not commercial) you can be bothered by visits from officials and perhaps fined and even shut down. Buying a local business permit may be enough to keep officials happy, but your state may also require licensing for you to sell any form of wildlife. This is a separate issue from a municipality business license.

How will your municipality and/or state wildlife officers know you're offering young

## Combat

During breeding season, and to a lesser degree at other times, male boas and pythons indulge in combat to establish dominance.

snakes for sale? They read the classified ads, ads in Kingsnake.com, and Craigslist.

**3.** Do you have the resources to take care of two dozen or more young snakes until you do sell them? This takes caging, food items, heating/cooling, and most of all, your time.

# Breeding

**Sexing:** To breed your snakes, you must have one of each sex. Compare the shape and length of the tail; to accommodate the hemipenes, the male's tail is broader at the base than that of a similarly sized female; it also tapers less abruptly and is comparatively longer. For boids, compare the size of the pelvic spurs, larger and longer in the male.

"Probing" is a more reliable way to sex subadult and adult snakes. Gently insert a lubri-

cated probe into the cloaca of the snake. If it is male, the probe will fit into the hemipenial pocket (see glossary, pages 108, 109) deeper than if inserted into a female. Learn to probe under the guidance of an experienced individual. If the probe is of incorrect diameter or is forced, injury may occur.

Newly hatched snakes may be sexed by manually everting the hemipenes of males, placing the thumb a few scales posterior to the vent and rolling the thumb firmly, but very gently, forward. Females have no hemipenes to evert. This technique must *never* be used on a hatchling green tree python because permanent tail kinking will occur. Ask an experienced individual to guide you.

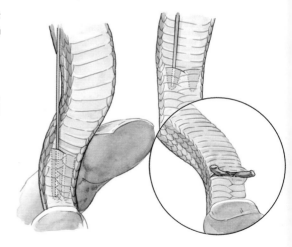

*Probing is the most reliable way of sexing an adult snake (male left, female right). Hatchlings (in circle) may be manually sexed (a male with everted hemipenes is depicted) but this should be done by an experienced person (not recommended for tree boas and green tree pythons).*

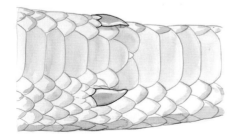

*The pelvic spurs of a male boid are typically larger than those of a female.*

## Cooling or Hibernation?

Most snakes need a wintertime cooling or hibernation to trigger breeding. (See individual species accounts.) Time the cooling to coincide with the coldest months in your area

A snake originating from a temperate area (some rat, king, and bullsnakes; some rosy, sand, and Argentine boas, among others) will require more and longer cooling than a species from a tropical area (such as boa constrictors), especially for captive-bred snakes . Their successive offspring do not seem to require such a precise cooling period.

## Winter Preparation for Cooling

**1.** Separate the sexes, except boa constrictors (genus *Boa*); many herpetoculturists suggest leaving them together.

**2.** Stop feeding two weeks prior to cooling.

**3.** Reduce relative humidity by cooling a room with air conditioning. Use a smaller water dish and remove plants from the cage.

**4.** Reduce photoperiod. Decrease the day length by 30 minutes each week.

**5.** Reduce temperature. Cool males to slightly lower temperatures than females. Daytime temperatures of 78–83°F (26–28°C) and nighttime temperatures of 69–73°F (21–23°C) are usually adequate. After a 90-day resting period, prepare for spring.

## Spring Preparation

**1.** Increase photoperiod by 30 minutes each week.

**2.** Increase temperature.

**3.** Increase relative humidity.

**4.** Once the snakes are alert, offer food (once they feed, offer again in three weeks).

**5.** Put the sexes together.

**6.** A gentle misting (simulating rain) may stimulate your snake's reproductive behavior. A simple spray bottle works fine, aimed high so the mist falls like a gentle rain.

**7.** Place a second sexually mature male in the cage. The territoriality response often turns to reproductive interest, but be prepared to intervene and remove the second specimen.

Some snakes (boids especially) are more aggressive during the breeding season, even specimens that have never displayed any hostility toward other snakes or their keepers. Remember this if your snake is large. Gravid or incubating female boids of some species will become belligerent to all intruders.

# Gestation and Egg Deposition

Gestating snakes need rather warm, secure areas for basking and egg deposition (or in the case of ovoviviparous species, to give birth).

*Covered plastic shoe or sweater boxes serve well as hibernating receptacles. An anthill python is shown.*

## Winter Hibernation (Not for Tropical Snakes)

**1.** Separate the sexes.

**2.** Stop feeding two weeks prior to hibernation, and do not feed during the hibernation period.

**3.** Reduce relative humidity by removing items from the cage that retain moisture, such as plants and the water dish. Unless you want to use the entire cage as a hibernaculum, offer a plastic container, such as a shoe box, as the hibernation quarters.

**4.** Clear a shelf in a cool, little-used closet in a basement or garage for the hibernation cage or box. Snakes need steady darkness and very cool temperatures for hibernation.

**5.** Hibernation temperatures should be between 48 and 56°F (9–13°C).

**6.** Rouse hibernating specimens for a drink about every 15 days. Take it out of its box,

place it on a shelf in front of you, and offer it water. After it drinks, place it back into its hibernation quarters. (Do not allow the snake to warm to room temperature.) If the snake does not drink, return it to its quarters and reoffer water in a week.

**7.** At the end of the hibernation period, replace your snake in its regular caging with water dish, hiding box, limbs and plants, etc.

**8.** Allow the snake(s) a week or so to wake up and warm up, then offer food.

**9.** A day after offering food, even if the snake has not eaten, put the sexes together. If courtship does not begin, mist the snakes gently, letting the mist fall like rain.

After mating, separate the snakes and offer another meal. Feed your snake(s) until they regain their prehibernation weight.

**The egg "box":** An opaque plastic dish partially filled with barely moistened, sterilized peat or sphagnum will often be accepted as a deposition site. This becomes even more desirable if it is covered, either by an opaque lid or by placing the tub in a darkened cardboard box. In both cases, cut an appropriately sized access hole. If the cage temperatures are cool, the deposition tub can be set on top of a heating cable or pad (set on low) to increase warmth. Heat from beneath will quickly dry the sphagnum (or other medium), and remoistening this will be necessary on a regular basis.

Females investigate their cages prior to deposition, looking for the best spot to lay eggs. Your female will probably spend time "resting" in the egg deposition tub before she actually places the eggs there. Some snakes will spend days in the tub, but lay their eggs in the water bowl. To avoid this, remove the water dish, only replacing it for an hour or so

*After having incubated for about 60 days at 80°F (27°C), this clutch of corn snake eggs has begun to hatch.*

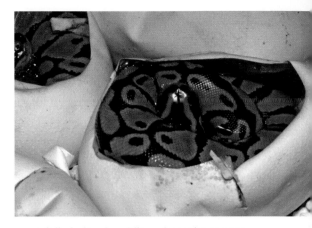

*About to hatch, the top of this egg was removed to show the baby ball python within.*

each evening. When the eggs are laid, mark the upper surface with a penciled "X." Move the eggs to the container which will be placed in the incubator, keeping the "X" side up. The egg container for the incubator can be a margarine tub or plastic shoebox filled with dampened, sterilized sphagnum moss. Keep the lid loosely on the container to maintain high humidity.

After egg deposition, offer the female food and step up the feedings. Females that retain or quickly regain their body weight following egg deposition will breed more frequently and successfully than underweight specimens or those slow to recover their weight.

## Incubation Procedures and Techniques

With oviparous snakes, incorrect temperatures during gestation and incubation can result in embryo deformity or death. Incubators can be homemade or purchased. Chick-egg incubators, with variable incubation temperature settings, from any feed store are big enough for several clutches of eggs and can be reused.

**Temperature:** The suggested incubation temperature is between 76 and 82°F (24–28°C). Humidity should be maintained at 80–95 percent. Keep an open container of water in the incubator. Keep it dark. Once laid, eggs may be gently moved but must not be turned. Frequent handling, rough handling, and excessively brilliant lighting are not good for the developing embryos. Although most neonates have no trouble escaping from the amniotic sac, weak babies might experience troubles,

especially in low humidity, where the sac rapidly dries and "toughens." If the baby seems unable to emerge, carefully rupture the membranous covering.

**Hatching:** Healthy, full-term young should emerge from their eggs after about 60 days without incident, slitting the egg with an egg-tooth on their upper lip and emerging within a day or two, peering out at intervals. In rare cases (such as when the egg membrane dries too quickly due to improper humidity), the babies may need a little help. Raising the relative humidity often seems to work. A short slit in the top of the egg or egg-membrane may also help. Be sure not to cut blood vessels.

**Caution:** If you slit an egg prematurely (sometimes only a few days) it may be fatal.

## Caution!

Captive-bred or captive-*kept* reptiles should never be released into the wild. Captive-produced reptiles are poor competitors, and there is the danger of introducing illnesses lethal to entire wild populations.

## Materials Needed for One Incubator

- 1 wafer thermostat/heater (You can find these at feed stores; these are commonly used in incubators for chicks)
- 1 thermometer
- 1 heat tape (obtained from hardware or garden stores)
- 1 Styrofoam cooler with thick sides—a fish shipping box is ideal

## Directions

**1.** Poke a hole through the lid of the styrofoam cooler, and suspend the thermostat/heater from the inside. Add another hole for a thermometer so you can simply pull it out to check the inside temperature without opening the top. If there's no flange on the thermometer to keep it from slipping through the hole in the lid, use a rubber band wound several times around the thermometer to form a flange.

**2.** Transverse the bottom of the cooler with the heat tape (don't let it cross itself) and wire the tape to the thermostat.

**3.** Put the lid of the cooler, and plug in the thermostat/heater. Wait half an hour

*An incubator may be made from a sturdy Styrofoam box, thermostat, and heating unit.*

then check the temperature. Adjust the thermostat/heater until the temperature inside the incubator is about 80° to 86°F (27–30°C). The L-pin "handle" on the top of the thermostat is the rheostat.

**4.** Once you have the temperature regulated, add your hardware cloth shelf. Your incubator is ready to go.

## Eureka! I have Eggs! Congratulations

**1.** Make certain the incubation medium—sphagnum moss or peat moss—in the egg container is damp. Cover the egg container and put it into the incubator. (If the eggs are piled too high to allow you to add the cover, cover the container with plastic wrap.) Be sure to put the cover back onto the incubator.

**2.** Check the temperature daily and adjust as needed (you shouldn't have to touch the thermostat, but check the temperature anyway, in case the thermostat goes rogue). Add a little water to the incubating medium as needed. The preferred humidity is 100%, which can be accomplished by keeping the incubation medium damp to the touch.

**3.** By the end of the first week, those eggs that are

# AN INCUBATOR

not fertile will turn yellow, harden, and begin to collapse. Those that are fertile will remain white and turgid to the touch. Infertile eggs may mold, but this is seldom transferred to healthy eggs.

**4.** At the end of the incubation period—which may be as little as two weeks for some species, but it is usually 60-70 days—the baby snakes will cut a slit in their egg with the egg tooth on the tip of their snout.

The babies usually are not eager to leave the egg. They will cut a slit, look out, and decide to stay inside the egg for a while longer, perhaps as long as a day and a half. Those that leave the egg can be removed to another terrarium and offered food, a sunning spot, a hiding spot, and water. They should shed within a few days, and feed a day or so after that.

Some of your young snakes may refuse to feed for no discernable reason. These young are simply called "nonfeeders," and even those who breed snakes for a living are at a loss for the reason. Watching a young snake slowly

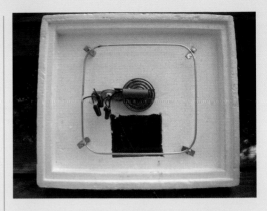

*The wafer thermostat and heating coil of an incubator must be of high quality and reliable.*

starve to death is sad and frustrating at the same time. Most of us try a few different food types, depending on the kind of snake, before we type the young as a nonfeeder. Then we put the snake in the freezer (one never, ever, turns loose a captive snake, no matter what the excuse).

# BOAS AND PYTHONS

*Boas and pythons, members of the family Boidae, are primarily tropical animals. A few of the smaller, secretive species occur in cool-to-cold temperate areas. Although some tropical species grow to immense sizes, most do not.*

Boas occur in deserts, savannas, woodlands, and rainforests. They may burrow, climb, or exploit ground surface habitats; one member, the anaconda, is primarily aquatic. Except for two endangered Indian Ocean island species, all boas are live-bearers.

With but a single exception, pythons are found in the Old World. Most are ground dwellers, but most also climb agilely. One is fossorial and another is primarily arboreal. Most are excellent swimmers. All are egg layers.

Boas and pythons are comparatively primitive snakes that retain pelvic remnants visible as movable anal spurs. The spurs of males are usually larger and are used in breeding stimulation and territorial disputes.

**A word of caution:** those who are thinking of acquiring one of the boa or python species that grow beyond a handleable length of eight feet (2.5 m) should carefully consider their acquisition. Snakes this large may not be legal

*Here is a beautiful red-tailed boa,* **Boa c. constrictor,** *in the Peruvian rain forest.*

in your area, can be dangerous if handled by a single individual, and are difficult to place if you decide to get rid of them.

## Boa Constrictor
### *Boa constrictor* ssp.

Mention the word "snake" to most people and the first image that comes to mind is the boa constrictor. Now scientifically designated *Boa constrictor* ssp. (the "ssp." stands for "subspecies"), these snakes were called *Constrictor constrictor* ssp. for many years.

In general, boa constrictors do very well in captivity. Freshly imported specimens may arrive with respiratory distress or mouth rot, but healthy, acclimated boas are resistant to most problems. Because the causes of respiratory infections and mouth rot can vary, and because cures are best determined following sensitivity tests, don't delay in getting assistance from a veterinarian.

It is only within the last decade that boas have been captive bred in any great numbers.

Since then, and many aberrant colors and patterns have been successfully produced.

## What Is a "Red-Tailed" Boa?

Although you can expect to pay more when buying particularly "pretty" examples of most snakes, price based on color is a fact in the boa constrictor market. As a rule, boas from the rain forests, and especially the Amazon Basin, have tails of a deeper red than boas from the drier areas. Referred to as "red-tailed boas" by dealers, these boas command proportionately high prices. Most are of the subspecies *B. c. constrictor*, the Amazon Basin boa.

## Common (or Colombian) Boa
### *B. c. imperator*

**Coloration:** Boas of this subspecies remain readily available. Those seen in the U.S. pet market are usually shipped from Colombia, and thus originate from the more colorful, most southerly populations of the race. They have a tan to warm brown ground color that deepens to orange or orange-red on the tail. *B. c. imperator* from Mexico and much of Central America are often of a much darker ground color and heavily peppered with black. As would be expected from a race that covers

*For more than 50 years, a small colony of boas, probably originating from the vicinity of Leticia, Colombia, has been established in Miami, Florida.*

such a vast north-south range, *B. c. imperator* is variable, not only in coloration, but in morphology. It has fewer than 253 ventral scales, and its dorsal scale rows, counted at midbody, number from 55–79. The dark-colored dorsal blotches from anterior nape to above the vent number 22 or more.

**Size:** They often attain lengths between 8 and 10 feet (2.5–3 m), but much larger sizes are documented. The largest authenticated boa of any subspecies was 18.5 feet (2.6 m).

**Range:** Southward from northern Mexico to the northern rim of the Amazon Basin.

**Comments:** Of the imported Colombian boas, many are now produced on "breeding farms." A greater number of common boas are now being captive bred than ever before. A common boa usually costs about $75. Unless, of course, you wish to indulge in "red-tailed" specimens (add $50) or albinos (add several thousand dollars).

At the southern end of the range, the **Argentine Boa** (*B. c. occidentalis*), indigenous to Paraguay and Argentina, is more tolerant of cool temperatures than its congeners.

Adult Argentine boas measure a little more than nine feet (2.7 m) in total length. The largest females produce the largest clutches, with babies sometimes numbering in the mid-50s. Smaller clutches have been produced by females as small as 6 feet (1.8 m) in length.

Adults of the Argentine boa are the darkest of all of the recognized boa subspecies. At one time, there was not much interest shown in them by hobbyists. It was not until several years after the exportation of these snakes was halted (in the formative years of herpetoculture), that hobbyists began to show a real interest in Argentine boas.

Newborn Argentines now range from $200–$350, depending on how many are actually available at any given time. Virtually all now available in the pet trade are the result of captive breeding programs.

**Other subspecies:** Other popular subspecies of the boa constrictor include the **Northwest Peruvian boa** (*B. c. ortonii*); the **Bolivian boa**, (*B. c. amarali*), and the **Hog Island** (Honduras) **boa** (*B. c. imperator*).

**Reproduction:** In the wild, a two- to three-month "rest period" of cooler or drier weather is followed by increased day length, relative humidity, and rainfall. These climatic changes trigger breeding activity. Some (and preferably all) of these criteria must be duplicated in captivity if you hope for breeding success.

Provide fewer hours of illumination and slightly cool your boas during your winter months. Nighttime lows of 69–73°F (21–23°C) for 6–12 weeks will be suitable. Daytime temperatures should range from 78 to 83°F (26–28°C). During this cooling period, also lower the cage humidity. Lowering humidity is most easily done by increasing ventilation within the cage (especially when your household furnace is on, which dramatically lowers available humidity) or by removing the water dish during the day. After the passing of the predetermined time,

*Nose to nose with a young Colombian boa.*

begin increasing photoperiod, warming, and raising the relative humidity in your boas' cage. This can be done gradually or at one time, as you prefer. After the boas are again active and the temperatures at their normal high, periodically mist the cage and the snakes.

Many persons prefer to keep the sexes separated except at breeding season. We have not found this to be a necessity. As a matter of fact, community breeding has proved more successful than individual projects. Heightened territorial and sexual activity can be induced by introducing a sexually adult male boa from another colony to the breeding cage. Use care when doing this; fights can ensue.

Despite our increased knowledge of their needs, the breeding of boas remains a difficult task. Captive-born specimens often breed more readily, and it may take wild-collected boas many years to acclimate sufficiently to breed in captivity. If you start out with immature captive-born boas, it will still take them several years to attain sexual maturity.

Bred females should have suitable warmth and an adequately large hiding area. A bask-

of small mammals and lizards. Of the 10 or more species (the number of species and sub-species has never been agreed on by authorities), only three or four are frequently seen in the European and American pet markets.

In general, sand boas are secretive snakes that are moderately flattened under normal conditions. When frightened or cold, they will laterally flatten their bodies even more to either seem more imposing to a predator or to present more surface for thermoregulation. They tend to lash sideways to bite until you pick them up. Sand boas are specifically adapted for a fossorial existence. They have an enlarged rostral scale, heads that are not distinct from their necks, and short tails and scales which are usually smooth anteriorly but often heavily keeled posteriorly.

In the wild, these snakes feed on lizards, other snakes, and small mammals. Neonates *may* occasionally eat an insect.

ing area with an air temperature of 92–95°F (33–35°C) and a substrate temperature (at the hot spot) of 94–105°F (34–41°C) will usually be used extensively by gestating female boas of all subspecies. Improper temperatures will often result in aborted undeveloped egg masses ("slugs") or partially developed young. Even a short period of improper temperature may result in aberrantly patterned or deformed young. The fact that many of the female boas imported while gravid either abort or birth deformed babies strongly suggests that gravid females should be disturbed as little as possible.

# Kenyan and Other Familiar Sand Boas
## Genera *Eryx* and *Gongylophis*

**Introduction:** Sand boas (subfamily Erycinae) are the Old World equivalents of the New World rosy and rubber boas. Primarily aridland snakes, they often seek refuge in the burrows

## Kenyan Sand Boa
### *Eryx colubrinus loveridgei*

Of all of the sand boa species, the East African Kenyan sand boa is most commonly seen in U.S. herpetoculture. It is no longer imported from the wild in any great numbers, and its availability is due to captive breeding.

**Coloration:** The Kenyan sand boa has some shades of orange, buff, or yellow dorsal and lateral markings against a brown or olive brown background color. The venter is off-white. Males tend to be more brilliantly colored

*This Kenyan sand boa is more brilliantly colored than many.*

than females. Albino and anerythristic strains are now being captive-bred. The albinos are patterned yellow or cream on white; the anerythristic strain is patterned with black against a light gray-blue ground color. Although both of these morphs are in demand by hobbyists, we continue to prefer the more commonly seen (and far less costly) normal phases.

**Range:** Found in Kenya and Tanzania.

**Size:** Adult female Kenyan sand boas are bulky and often reach 22–24 inches (56–61 cm) in length. Males are considerably smaller and of slighter build. Males may be identified by their proportionately longer and stouter tail and the larger cloacal spurs. This sand boa may deliver one or more slashing bites on provocation. However, once in hand they usually become quiet. Neonates are about eight inches (20 cm) long at birth and entirely ready to bite on emergence from the amniotic sac.

**Breeding:** An easily bred species, the Kenyan sand boa requires only moderate cooling to cycle reproductively. Simply offer a greater daytime thermal gradient and drop the nighttime temperature a few degrees for up to 90 days during the winter months, coupled with a reduction in photoperiod. Our snakes are "cooled" during December, January, and February. As we always do, we continue to provide the normal, seasonally variable, hours of daylight. During this time the daytime highs do not usually rise above the low eighties (27–29°C) and nighttime lows may drop into the mid 60s (18–20°C). It is not unusual for the boas to refuse most or all food during cooling. Because these snakes are normally a very

robust and hardy species, this seldom causes any problems. Breeding begins soon after the springtime elevation of the cage temperature.

They do well in trios (one male, two females). Young are produced annually. Parturition occurs about four to five months after breeding, in late summer or early autumn.

When our females were gravid, a heating pad (with the setting on low) was placed beneath half of the terrarium and run continuously. Except for the hottest days, when in late afternoon the summer sun would warm the entire room to the high eighties or low nineties (31–34°C), the females chose to have at least part of their bodies in the warmed sand atop the pad.

Clutch size may vary from 3 and 22 (usually 10 to 16) rather hefty babies. Although a few of the neonates may insist on lizards for their first meal, the vast majority will accept newly born mice. Even the lizard eaters will soon switch over to mice, especially if the pinkies are scented with lizard odor. Several of our neonates have eaten crickets that accidentally got into their cage, but we can find no reference to insects being included in the diet of wild specimens. One of the Kenyans that accepted several crickets was a neonate that had refused to eat anything we offered. After eating several crickets, the little snake ate a cricket-scented pinky mouse and then readily began accepting normal, unscented pinkies.

**Caging:** A terrarium made from a 20-gallon (76 L) "long" aquarium is ideal for three small boids. The substrate was of three to five inches (8–13 cm) of dry builder's sand. (Do note that sand is a very heavy medium. Be certain that your terrarium's stand can hold the weight.) A small untippable dish of clean water was presented to the boas for about two days once every week or two. The boas would usually investigate the dish soon after it was in place, but only sometimes drink.

Normally, summer daytime temperatures ranging from the mid-80s (28–29°C) to the mid-90s (34–36°C) are ideal. A heating pad or a heat tape beneath one end of the terrarium will provide a thermal gradient.

Provide summer day temperatures of 92–96°F (33–36°C) on the hot end of the terrarium, and allow to cool it at night to as low as the mid- to low seventies (21–25°C).

Like other erycine species, much of its moisture requirements are apparently metabolized from food animals. Adults are usually ravenous feeders on lab mice or rat pups.

## Rough-Scaled Sand Boa
### G. conicus

Next to the Kenyan sand boa, the rough-scaled sand boa is the best known and one of the calmest of the pet trade erycines.

**Coloration:** Against the tan, buff, gray, or yellowish ground color are three rows of dark spots, one on each side and a particularly broad series dorsally. The dark markings may vary from reddish brown to deep rich chocolate brown to nearly black. The spots may fuse into bars or a very broad and irregular vertebral stripe. The head bears prominent postorbital stripes.

**Size:** Females of this very heavy-bodied sand boa may attain, or even slightly exceed, a two-foot (61 cm) body length. Males are smaller.

**Range:** This savanna dweller is common to areas of India, Pakistan, Sri Lanka, and adjacent countries.

**Breeding:** This species seems to require considerable cooling to breed successfully. Captives can be bred annually, but a biennial breeding sequence may be more normal in the wild.

This species has fairly small clutches (normally three to nine, but sometimes more) of

*Gongylophis conicus, an Asiatic species, is commonly known as the rough-scaled sand boa.*

*Some smooth-scaled sand boas, Eryx johni, remain brightly colored, but most assume an overall brown color when adult.*

rather large young. The neonates will usually accept pinky (or slightly larger) mice. (See also the breeding comments for the next species.)

**Caging:** Although less persistent and gifted burrowers than other members of the genus, they do thrive in a "normal" sand boa setup.

## Smooth-Scaled Sand Boa
### *E. johnii*

The smooth-scaled sand boa is less commonly available than the Kenyan sand boa.

**Coloration and appearance:** The adults often have a dull brown coloration, but juveniles (and some adults) have varied colors. These latter have broad dark bands crossing a ground color of orange. David Sorenson, one of the premier breeders of this species in the United States, believes that pattern expression is populational at best rather than subspecific.

In gross appearance, the smooth-scaled sand boa resembles the American rubber boa. Both have a narrow head, loose skin, and a bluntly rounded tail, but the smooth-scaled sand boa has a greatly enlarged rostral scale.

**Size:** The smooth-scaled sand boa is one of the larger members of the genus, reaching or even exceeding, three feet (.9 m) in length.

**Range:** This species is found in India, Pakistan, Bangladesh, and Iran.

**Breeding:** Like many other sand boas, this is a hardy and easily maintained species, which rarely attempts to bite. *E. johnii* is seldom bred successfully and seems to require a lengthy period of almost complete hibernation, with temperatures as low as 58–62°F (14–17°C)

easily sustained by these snakes. The neonates number from two to eight and are quite large and well able to eat pinky (or slightly larger) mice. Despite its reputation for hardiness, the infrequency with which this species is bred indicates that hobbyists still need to learn more about its basic necessities.

**Caging:** Except when in hibernation, *E. johnii* requires temperatures near 95°F (35°C) during the day but which drop by about 10°F at night. We always provide thermal gradients, with the cool end of the terrarium being room temperature (about 84°F [29°C] by day and slightly cooler at night).

# Rainbow Boas

## Brazilian Rainbow Boa
### *Epicrates c. cenchria*

Although the genus *Epicrates* contains many species of West Indian boas, it is the tropical American rainbow boas that are most favored by hobbyists. Of these, the Brazilian and the lookalike Peruvian are the most popular, followed by the Argentine and the Colombian.

At present, the importation of wild specimens of these beautiful boas has all but ceased. Because of this more limited availability, prices have climbed, with, as expected, the most attractive specimens of the Brazilian rainbow boa being the most expensive.

**Color and identifying characteristics:**
Although variably colored, the ground coloration of the Brazilian rainbow boa is brighter than that of any other. The dorsal and dorsolateral surfaces are clad in scales of rich oranges or orange-browns. Large dorsal ocelli, prominently outlined in dark brown or black, are present. These may abut or be narrowly separated from one another. The lateral surfaces are lighter and prominent black blotches, bordered above by a crescent of pink or buff (which is edged with black). The iridescent highlights

*The Peruvian rainbow boa (pictured here) and the Brazilian rainbow boa are of very similar appearance.*

**Comments:** The several races of rainbow boas are hardy and easily maintained, although they tend to be "snappy." The more tropical varieties can catch respiratory ailments if temperatures are low while humidity in their cages is high. In most cases, "drier is better" at cooler temperatures.

Adult rainbow boas will eat rats, mice, chicks, and small guinea pigs.

from which the common name of "rainbow boa" are derived are particularly well developed in this race. Dark postorbital and midcranial stripes are nearly equally prominent. The neonates are less richly colored than the adults.

**Range and habitat:** This race is encountered in tropical Brazil and contiguous regions of adjacent countries. Although terrestrial (but well able to climb), these snakes may be found in river, swamp, and pond edge habitats as well as in sclerophyll woodland, thornscrub, and rain forest. Rainbow boas are often found in and near village dumping areas due to the abundance of rodent prey.

**Size:** The Colombian and Brazilian races often exceed a hefty six-foot (1.8 m) length (and sometimes exceed eight feet [2.5 m]), whereas the Argentine rainbow boa is of more slender build and is rarely more than six feet (1.8 m) in length.

**Breeding:** From six to more than 20 live young are produced either annually or biennially, depending on the fecundity of the female. The neonates are often aggressive, rather large, and will usually readily feed on small mice. Although they begin breeding late in life, they are not difficult to breed in captivity.

Reproductive behavior is stimulated in the normal manner—separate the sexes (optional), then reduce temperature, photoperiod, and humidity. After six to eight weeks, the temperature, photoperiod, and relative humidity are again elevated, and the two sexes placed together. Breeding will often quickly ensue.

**Other subspecies:** The **Argentine rainbow boa,** *E. c. alvarezi,* is the southernmost subspecies of the genus. It occurs in southern Brazil, Paraguay, and Argentina. Although pretty, the Argentine rainbow boa is not as richly and contrastingly colored as the Brazilian. The ground colors of the Argentine rainbow boa are tans and buffs. It is darkest dorsally. The dorsal saddles are narrowly outlined in dark brown and the light centered lateral spots are poorly defined. Dark postorbital stripes and a less prominent midcranial stripe are present. Neonates are much more brilliantly colored.

**Comments:** Unlike its more tropical congenerics, cooler winter temperatures are needed to breed the Argentine rainbow boa.

The **Colombian rainbow boa,** *E. c. maurus,* ranges southward from Costa Rica to Colombia and may be found in contiguous areas of abutting countries as well. Adults are russet to brown, and neither dorsal nor lateral blotches are much in evidence. The neonates are much more brilliantly colored and look very much like a pale version of the Brazilian rainbow boa. Like others of the genus, the Colombian rainbow boa assumes a lighter color at night.

*This is a pair of rosy boas,*
*Lichanura trivirgata saslowi,*
*from mid-Baja California.*

# New World Erycines

## Rosy Boas
*Lichanura trivirgata* ssp.

**Introduction:** In many ways, rosy boas are the perfect boa because they are small, pretty, interesting but secretive, and hardy.

Rosy boas range from central western Arizona and southern California to northwestern Mexico and over much of the Baja, to the southernmost tip. They are also found on a few islands off both Baja coasts. They frequently live in rocky hillsides, mountains, and canyons. Many of these areas have vast expanses of sandy desert that serve as barriers to prevent them wandering from canyon to canyon.

Different populations have specific color patterns. Those from Baja have a steel gray body and narrow, precise striping (*L. t. saslowi*). Those from Arizona have wide rust stripes on dusky gray background (*L. t. gracia*). Certain subtleties may be quite restricted. Thus, it is rather an easy matter for an experienced researcher or hobbyist to guess the origin of a given specimen. Expertise may be *so* well

*This is a pair of albino coastal rosy boas.*

In mid-February, the snakes are brought out of hibernation or cooling, and photoperiod is increased to that which is naturally occurring outside. After a few days of warmth, the snakes are fed a small meal.

It is important that adults be of ample weight before breeding because males and females routinely fast. This voluntary fasting *may* last several weeks. Males may not feed again until a week or two after the end of the breeding season. Some females may feed once or twice after having been bred; others continue to eat throughout their gestation.

If kept communally, they will breed when ready. If kept separately, introduce the females to the males after several meals. During courtship, the male zigzags himself atop the female and stimulates her with his cloacal spurs.

Gestation averages about four months. Females usually undergo a "prenatal shed" from several weeks to as little as one week prior to parturition. A day or so before parturition, females will usually begin restlessly prowling their cages.

An average litter consists of five to eight young that may vary in size from about 10 to slightly more than 14 inches (25–36 cm) in total length. Babies can be short tempered and very hostile at even the most benign of human overtures. With growth and gentle handling, most will eventually quiet.

**Habitat:** Snakes of semiarid, rocky, and boulder-strewn habitats near desert springs, streams, and canyon seepages, they may be found from sea level to more than 4,000 feet in elevation. They wander both day and night, and may be found crossing roadways in the

honed that the origin of the snake can be narrowed to a particular canyon!

We strongly urge that you retain the characteristics of the various phases and subspecies by breeding only within the same population. Most hobbyists enjoy knowing the particular canyon that their specimen is from. Intergrades and muddled morphs—"mutts" if you will—are of far less interest to advanced hobbyists.

**Size:** Rosy boas are robust. Their tail is heavy but not bluntly rounded. Adults are about 30 inches (76 cm) in length. They mature quickly, and at about two years old they produce small litters of large young.

**Breeding:** Rosy boas are not difficult to breed. They may be kept communally (a pair or trio) throughout the year or housed singly. Females may be sequentially introduced to a male's container. There are several methods of cycling, all with a similar success rate. Some breeders believe they do best if fully hibernated for two to three months. Others merely allow a substantial cooling, during which the snake receives only eight hours of daylight.

late winter and early spring. Hot weather usually induces crepuscular and nocturnal activity or lengthy periods of inactivity.

**Caging:** In most areas of the country, rosy boas are wonderfully hardy little snakes. In the deep (and perpetually humid) southeast, they seem sometimes to develop regurgitation syndrome, especially when the high humidity is accompanied by lower than optimum temperatures. An abnormal proliferation of gut protozoans may also contribute to the problem. Regurgitation *may* be corrected by elevating cage temperatures to 88–92°F (31–33°C) and by lowering relative humidity. To keep humidity low, we suggest placing the water dish in the cage for a few hours only once every two to three weeks. If regurgitation continues, veterinary assessment should be sought. If left untreated, the snakes will weaken and die.

Rosy boas are easily handled snakes. Many live for more than 15 years in captive life. With increasing knowledge, we expect the average captive lifespan to increase; others in this subfamily routinely exceed 25 years.

# Two Popular New World Tree Boas

## Emerald Tree Boa
### *Corallus caninus*
**Color and identifying characteristics:** In color, adult emerald tree boas are emerald green. The only relief from the green occurs as an occasional yellow scale and a series of variable enamel-white dorsal bars. The venter, and sometimes the lips, are yellow or whitish. Color alone will identify the adults of this species. Neonate emeralds may be harder to

identify because at birth they are often brick-red in color, but still with conspicuous white vertebral markings. Within a very short time, an overall green suffusion becomes apparent. The emerald is the only New World tree boa species to undergo radical ontogenetic changes (those changes associated with age). Amazon Basin specimens are more intensely colored than specimens from elsewhere in the range.

**Size:** This boa is, for its six-foot (1.8 m) (plus) length, a powerful, predatory constrictor of proportionately stocky build. Anchored securely to its supporting limb by a strong prehensile tail, it can first strike, then drop powerful constricting coils from its leafy bower to overpower its prey of birds and small mammals.

*Orange when born, the color of this Amazon Basin emerald tree boa will soon change to leaf green.*

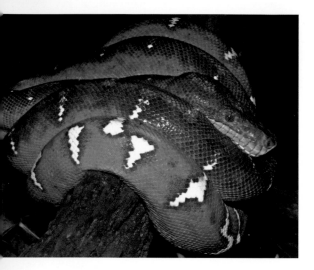

*Although not always easy to acclimate to captive conditions, emerald tree boas, **Corallus caninus**, are coveted snakes. This is an adult from Suriname.*

decrease prey size even more. Using such care, Chiras has never lost an emerald.

**Caging:** We suggest that vertically oriented caging, replete with horizontal perches of a diameter about equal to that of the snake's body, be used for this beautiful serpent. We disagree strongly with the current trend of using perches constructed of PVC, preferring instead fitted limbs with bark or grapevines. Boas are much more at ease with these naturalistic perches than with the smooth, difficult-to-hold PVC. The caging used for the emeralds is similar to that described for the Amazon tree boas (see page 48).

**Range and habitat:** Of the neotropical tree boas, the emerald is the most persistently arboreal. Although juveniles are usually found close to the ground, adult emeralds are considered a canopy species.

**Reproduction:** This ovoviviparous species usually produce less than 12 proportionately large babies. Once fully acclimated to your area, adults can be cycled by reducing winter temperature, humidity, and photoperiod. A nighttime temperature should drop to about 70–72°F (21–22°C). Daytime highs can be a few degrees warmer, and a hot spot of about 82°F (28°C) can be provided. Breeding will often begin with the lengthening photoperiods, increased humidity, and warming spring temperatures. Misting them will provide an added incentive. Although most will bite with only a small provocation, breeding males can be *very* aggressive. Use care when handling.

**Regurgitation:** Among the most perplexing of captive snakes, many specimens develop a tendency to regurgitate their prey if stressed in the least. The initial regurgitation may be triggered by incorrect temperatures, fright, the introduction of a new boa to the cage, shipping, an oversized meal, or several other causes. Once regurgitation has started, it can be difficult (but is seldom impossible) to stop.

Stan Chiras, a successful breeder of this species, suggests that cage temperatures for this species be kept in the 68–78°F (20–26°C) range. Cage humidity should be high. Once regurgitation has begun, feeding attempts should be reduced to once every two or three weeks and prey size also reduced (a half-grown mouse for an adult emerald). The goal is to get the digestive system functioning again, with as little stress as possible. There is a possibility that a gut stimulant may help digestion (check with your reptile veterinarian). If lucky, regurgitation will cease after the first try. If not, lengthen the span to the next attempt and

Although once common in the pet trade, by the early 1990s, extensive permitation procedures and seldom-granted permits restricted their importation. Because of their scarcity in the pet trade, they are very expensive. Captive-born neonates may cost $750 or more.

**Feeding:** It may take considerable experimentation to induce an adult to feed. It seems that they are not only prey specific, but many are color specific as well. Emeralds will usually eat hamsters, white mice, brown mice, white rats, brown rats, gerbils, baby chicks, and baby quail. Neonates and juveniles are more easily acclimated to captive diets.

Until fully accustomed to captive conditions, their cage should be placed in quiet surroundings, and the snakes given ample cover. Easily stressed, emeralds are more of a display snake than a pet snake.

Imported specimens are often heavily parasitized. Have a veterinarian assess the gut flora and fauna. A proliferation can cause repeated regurgitation and, if not curtailed, death.

## Amazonian Tree Boa
### C. hortulana ssp.

**Color and identifying characteristics:** The Amazonian tree boa is the most variable of the tree boas in both coloration and pattern. Hobbyists often refer to those with darker ground colors and silvery to buff pattern components as the garden phase. Amazonian tree boas may be gray, tan, olive, yellow, orange, or orange-red ground color. Some light specimens have well-defined darker markings, some dark specimens have well-defined light markings, some may be patterned with wide bands of yellow or pale green, some may be flecked, and some may be nearly unicolored. Most specimens have some black or dark brown radiations near the eyes. Hobbyists eagerly seek the reddest and yellowest of these tree boas. As with many other snakes, the most attractive snakes command the highest prices.

**Size:** Although this species may equal or even exceed the length of the emerald boa,

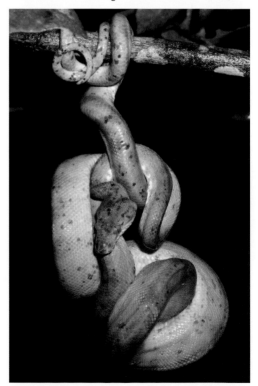

*This Amazon tree boa hangs from its strongly muscled and very prehensile tail.*

*Although often quite dull in color, some Amazon tree boas, Corallus hortulana, are remarkably beautiful.*

the lesser body bulk makes the Amazonian tree boa look considerably smaller. This tree boa can exceed seven feet (2.1 m) in length.

**Range and habitat:** Found over much of tropical South America, they can be particularly abundant in riveredge shrubbery, in public gardens, and in other cultivated areas. Most seem to be at home at the 4-to 15-foot (1.2–4.6 m) level in the vegetation. Juveniles are often found very low to the ground, and occasionally adults may descend to the ground.

**Breeding:** Large numbers (10–20) of live young are produced, and they have been repeatedly bred by herpetoculturists. The goal seems to be the reddest possible coloration.

We have seen gravid females in shipments of imported specimens throughout the summer months. Those we have bred have done so after having had temperature, humidity, and photoperiod reduced for the winter. Breeding commenced when all of these three components were increased and when gentle daily mistings were begun. Amazonian tree boas maintained outdoors in southwest Florida seemed stimulated to breed by the reduced barometric pressure that heralded the advent of a thunderstorm or frontal system.

**Caging:** Although an Amazonian tree boa can curl up in a remarkably small space, we suggest a vertically oriented cage of fair size. When indoors, our boas were maintained in cages that measured 5.5 feet (1.7 m) high and that had a floor space of $2 \times 3$ feet ($61 \times 91.4$ cm). The indoor cages were made of plywood and had a full-length glass front that opened for access. The cage was criss-crossed with horizontal branches. Live philodendrons and pothos served both as cover for the snakes and raised the cage humidity. When outside, the tree boas were in cages of similar size as when indoors, but the outdoor cages were made of wood frames that were covered with 1/8 inch (3 mm) mesh-welded wire to allow unfiltered sunlight and rain to enter.

**Comments:** These boas tend to be snappy and adjust poorly to handling. Of the four New World tree boa species, the Amazonian race of the garden tree boa seems the hardiest at all stages of its life. Neonates will often accept small hopper mice as their first meals, if teased with the morsel until they strike and constrict it. Holdouts will nearly always "break" on tree frogs or lizards, then after a few meals of these natural foods, accept fuzzy mice. Adults generally feed on laboratory mice.

# Ball Python
## *Python regius*

This python is one of the most commonly seen species in the American pet trade. It makes a calm, easy-going pet. When frightened, the ball python has the habit of rolling into a tight ball with its head hidden near the center of the protecting body coils.

**Coloration:** Ball pythons are normally available in black and tan coloration. Other colors are also available, including **golden**, axanthic (lacking yellow), striped, a yellow and brown **"jungle" phase**, and **piebald** and **albino** phases. Unlike the normal phase imports that may sell for less than $50 each, these special color phases may cost several thousand dollars each! Before you buy one of these unusually colored ball pythons, be aware that, in at least some cases, unusual colors may be temperature-derived oddities caused by high incubation temperatures.

**Behavior:** Although more terrestrial than most pythons, the ball python will occasionally climb to considerable heights. Adaptable in the wild, it is found in scrub, semiaridland and agricultural habitats. When hunting, ball pythons frequently follow rodents and other small mammals far back into their burrows.

**Appearance:** The head of the ball python is broad and distinct from the neck. Heat-sensitive labial (lip) pits are present. This is a small but heavy bodied snake. It is known to attain a maximum length of about six feet (1.8 m), though most adults are between 3.5 and

*Although ball pythons of normal coloration are inexpensive, some designer colors cost thousands of dollars.*

## Caution

A python of just eight feet (2.5 m) can kill a human toddler by asphyxiation and should not be handled by one individual. Pythons and some other snakes may be illegal in your area.

4.5 feet (1–1.4 m). Even at this smaller size they are of impressive girth.

**Availability:** Ball pythons are one of the more readily available and inexpensive python species offered in the U.S. pet trade. Ball pythons were once as readily available in most European countries as in America, but the sale of wild-collected snakes has been mainly curtailed throughout much of Europe.

**Origin:** Most ball pythons in pet markets are from tropical western Africa. Unfortunately, 99 percent of these snakes are either straight from the wild or are captive-hatched from eggs laid by wild-collected females. Upwards of 40,000 (and probably close to double that

*Albinism was one of the first designer colorations to appear in the ball python.*

number) ball pythons are imported annually for the American pet trade.

**Feeding:** Typically, ball pythons stop feeding during the winter (their dry season). Reproductively active adults may also stop feeding during the breeding season. Female ball pythons usually refuse food when gestating and incubating. Long-term captives, including captive-hatched examples, may fast during these periods.

In addition to their seasonal fasts, ball pythons are noted for "prey imprinting." That is, they want only the particular kind of prey animal they fed on in the wild. This may be a gerbil or an obscure rodent species not available here. Such snakes may hold out until nearly starved before accepting a commercially available rodent.

If you have a wild-collected ball python that refuses to eat, you may be battling a dietary preference or a normal feeding cessation. For these reasons, we strongly urge you to avoid this sort of frustration by purchasing only a ball python—hatchling or adult—you have seen feed.

If you are having a problem getting your ball python to eat, experiment with all types and colors of available food species—try gerbils (although our pet gerbil is not the same gerbil that is the ball python's natural prey), mice, small rats, and hamsters; try various colors; try all both alive and pre-killed. When you attempt the live prey, introduce it alive (*do not* leave the live prey unattended) in the early evening. When you try dead prey, first warm it (not in a microwave oven!) to normal body temperature, then place it in the door of your snake's hide box. Exposing the brain of a pre-killed animal may induce your snake to eat.

Ball pythons are capable of maintaining extended fasts with no permanent impairment. Some specimens have refused to eat for a year or more before breaking their fast. A fast of this duration may actually be more taxing on the snake's owner than on the snake.

*At the time that this photo was taken, this color phase of the ball python had not yet been named.*

**Longevity:** Despite the dietary problems that prevail with many freshly imported specimens, acclimated ball pythons can be hardy, easily kept, and long-lived snakes. Longevity records note a captive life of 20–47 years!

**Caging:** Because they are quite inactive, even adult ball pythons may be kept in relatively small cages. A cage with a floor space of 18 × 36 inches (46 × 91 cm) is large for a single adult snake or for even a pair of average-sized snakes.

Despite being heavy bodied, ball pythons can climb adeptly. We therefore provide a minimum cage height of two feet (60 cm) and elevated perches. We also provide two hide boxes in each cage—one positioned over and warmed by a heating pad and the other at the cool end of the cage. During cooler weather, most ball pythons preferentially choose the heated hide (this is especially true of gravid females), but may thermoregulate by moving with some degree of frequency from one to the other.

**Breeding and sexing:** Acclimated ball pythons are not very difficult to breed. Like all short-tailed python species, however, they **can** be tough to sex properly. Probing seems to be the most definitive method, but even this can be inconclusive sometimes.

Cycling your ball pythons for breeding is accomplished in the same manner as with other pythons and boas. The snakes should be well fed and heavy bodied, but not fat. Adequate body weight is important because sexually active (or receptive) ball pythons may decline food, often for many weeks.

Begin the breeding sequence by separating the sexes and reducing the winter cage temperature, photoperiod, and relative humidity. During the cooling period, a daytime high of

*Piebaldism is eagerly sought in ball pythons.*

76–80°F (24–27°C) and a nighttime low of 68–70°F (20–21°C) will suffice.

After six to eight weeks, elevate all of the climatic factors to their normal summer levels and place the sexes back together. With luck, breeding will soon begin. To stimulate breeding activity even further, you may temporarily place a second sexually mature male specimen with the pair. Territorial defense will usually ensue, often changing to a breeding response along the way. An occasional gentle misting, especially during barometric changes, may also provide desired stimulation.

Ball pythons lay small clutches (one to nine, usually three to six) of large eggs. At a temperature of 88–92°F (31–33°C) (with a relative humidity of 82–95 percent) incubation will last for about 2 months.

With time, captive breeding programs will provide us with an increasing number of domestically raised specimens. This will lessen the pressures of the pet industry to obtain wild-collected specimens.

In addition, as more are produced, the price of aberrant specimens will diminish somewhat. However, because ball pythons have very small clutches, it may be many years before some of the more unusual variants drop sufficiently in price to become regular pet-market items.

# Children's Python
## Antaresia (Liasis) maculosus

**Coloration:** This interesting little constrictor has a ground color of variable olive tan, or reddish-brown against which the very irregular brownish to reddish-brown dorsal and lateral blotches contrast strongly.

**Size:** This species reaches a rather slender 30 inches (76 cm).

**Range and habitat:** This is a woodland, forest, and semiaridland species of eastern and northcentral Australia.

**Breeding:** An easily bred small python that lays clutches of from 2–12 fairly large eggs, it usually require only a slight reduction of winter temperature concurrent with a lowered humidity to cycle. The eggs are easily incubated, hatching about two months after deposition (when incubated at 85–90°F [29–32°C]). Hatchlings usually feed readily on pinky mice.

Remarkably calm, hardy, and temperature-tolerant, its diminutive size allows a pair or a trio to be kept in a 30-gallon (114 L) terrarium. They feed readily on mice and newly born rats.

# Anthill Python
## Antaresia perthensis

The anthill python, also called the Perth python and the pygmy python, occurs in the Pilbara region of midwestern Western Australia. Despite its species name (which refers to the city of Perth, located on the south coast of Western Australia), the actual range of this tiny, interesting python is far to the north of its namesake city. Once thought a relict, dwarfed variety of the Children's python, the anthill python is now recognized as a full species. At an adult length of 20 to 28 inches (51–71 cm), this denizen of aridland western Australia is the smallest of the known pythons.

Anthill pythons apparently inhabit areas of red soil and are themselves of one or more shades of red. Young pythons often have well-defined dark red markings against a lighter ground color. The dark markings may obscure with advancing age.

*Children's python (named for a person), Antaresia childreni, is the most often seen species of the genus.*

*Adult at a mere 26 inches (66 cm),* **Antaresia perthensis,** *the antill python, is the smallest python known.*

A slight winter cooling will enhance the likelihood of breeding success. At a temperature of 82–84°F (28–29°C) the two to eight eggs (most often four to six) will hatch following an incubation duration of 54 to 60 days. Hatchlings are a slender six inches (15.25 cm) long.

Hatchlings can be picky feeders. They are barely large enough to eat the smallest pinky mice, and many will accept these as their initial prey. However, others will refuse rodents and hold out for small geckos—not always a readily available prey item. When considering a purchase of this comparatively expensive little snake, it is always a good idea to not only ask the breeder whether the pythons are voluntarily eating, but to also confirm what prey item they are accepting. Many breeders prefer to offer the little pythons pinky heads rather than the entire animal.

*The common name of anthill python is derived from the preferred habitat of this species, the big termite mounds ("anthills") of western Australia.*

# West African Burrowing Python
## *Calabaria reinhardtii*

**Coloration:** The ground color of the burrowing python is deep reddish-brown to bluish-black. Irregular patches of orangish to pinkish spots and blotches are present. Opalescent highlights are obvious. When entering the shed cycle, burrowing pythons become a translucent silvery-black.

The blunt, club-shaped tail is dark (often black) with conspicuous white subcaudal blotches. When the snake is balled up in a defensive posture, its tail is usually well in evidence, often protruding boldly outward from the tight coil of the body. This posture is a common protective ploy for blunt-tailed snakes of several families. The supposition is that an antagonist would then worry about the exposed tail and ignore the hidden head. Despite their shyness, they never bite.

The burrowing python has a gently rounded, enlarged rostral scale and a supple, well-muscled, cylindrical body shape. The head is not distinct from the neck. The scales are smooth.

The eyes are comparatively small, somewhat protuberant, and have an elliptical pupil.

**Range:** Forested areas of tropical West Africa.

**Food:** Some will accept suitably sized lab mice, but many prefer newly born rats.

**Caging:** Because it is a small, quiet, and secretive species, burrowing pythons do not require large cages. We keep our burrowing pythons in a 20-gallon (76 L) terrarium with a substrate consisting of several inches of barely moistened, loamy soil over which is a layer of fallen leaves one to two inches (2.5–5 cm) thick. These snakes are well adapted to dig burrows of their own, and are also able to utilize the burrows of small rodents. As often as not, our burrowing pythons are found lying beneath the leaves, but atop the soil, in their terrarium. A small, untippable water bowl should be present, and the humidity in the terrarium should be kept high but not saturated.

**Breeding:** Captive burrowing pythons have proved difficult to cycle reproductively. Although some hobbyists suggest that a period of cooling and fasting is required to effect the reproductive cycling of burrowing pythons, this seems unlikely. Others hobbyists suggest that the reproductive cycling of *Calabaria* is induced by varying humidity and substrate moisture levels. Considering the tropical forest humus habitat of this snake, it seems likely that the latter would be the *major* determi-

*Secretive and shy, the West African burrowing python won't spend much time away from cover in its caging.*

**Comments:** As with any snakes that are wild-collected and imported as adults, it has been difficult to determine the life expectancy of *Calabaria*. Wild specimens, age unknown, have lived for more than six years and some to about 10 years as captives. Now that we have captive-hatched babies to monitor, it seems likely that we will find that *Calabaria* are not only hardy, but at least as long-lived as some of the smaller erycine boas. We have found that if cage temperatures drop too near or below the mid-70s (21–24°C), *Calabaria* are apt to regurgitate their meals. The larger the meal fed when temperatures are cool, the more likely the snake is to regurgitate. Thus, even here in Florida, we now keep an undertank heating unit in place beneath one end of the terrarium. In all but the very warmest weather, we provide a thermal gradient for the snakes. The hot end of the terrarium is retained at between 87° and 90°F (31–32°C); the cool end is usually at ambient room temperature, but never below 78°F (26°C).

nant. However, when moisture and humidity levels are reduced (even in tropical forests, as during a naturally occurring dry season), temperatures often do drop somewhat. Although this natural reduction of temperature and humidity may not induce a cessation of feeding by the inhabitants, the creatures *may* feed somewhat less often. We do suggest that captive *Calabaria* be fed throughout the year, including during their gestation period.

Hobbyists may eventually find that a combination of *slight* cooling and reduced humidity for 30–45 days, followed by warming and increased humidity, might cycle *Calabaria*

more reliably than either method alone. Humidity can be elevated and retained by frequent gentle mistings of the substrate surface with tepid water.

Females lay from one to five (often three) large, elongated eggs. Varying from 10–12 inches (25–30 cm) in length, the hatchlings are far less retiring than the wild adults and are kept in a utilitarian terrarium, with only newspaper for a substrate. In such a habitat, the little snakes thrive, accepting mice from your fingers. A burrowing medium is not necessary (but a high humidity is).

Eggs incubated at temperatures between 87° and 90°F have hatched in approximately 50 days. A baby that hatched after 88 days from an egg incubated at "room temperature" (about 81–84°F) was undersized and had spinal kinks. It was euthanized, and an incubator was employed for eggs which followed. Hatchlings seem to show little balling (defensive) reaction when gently handled.

# Carpet Pythons
## *Morelia spilota* ssp.

Before the early 1970s, when Australia began to prohibit exportation of native wildlife, the carpet and the diamond pythons were commonly seen in the United States pet trade. At the time, wild-collected carpet pythons sold for $15–$20 each, and the diamond pythons for $30–$40.

Then, carpet and diamond pythons were suddenly no longer available in the United States. A few were present in zoological collections, an additional few remained in private collections. It is from these few snakes, along with occasional imports from European hobbyists, that today's ready availability has evolved.

Captive breeding of these snakes does have a disadvantage. Hobbyists can easily bring together snakes from widely disparate geographical origins. When these snakes are bred, however, you no longer have young snakes from northern Australia or a snake from a tiny valley in eastern Australia. Instead, you have a batch of intergrades. We strongly urge hobbyists to retain the integrity of the many phases of carpet python. It is only by breeding the various phases in the purest possible form that we will preserve the diversity of color now associated with this snake.

## Coastal Carpet Python
### (*M. s. mcdowelli*)

This subspecies is the most commonly seen carpet python in U.S. herpetoculture and the largest of the carpet pythons. It is large, robust, vigorous, and hardy. Although the adults of many populations seldom exceed 7 feet (2.1 m), those of others regularly grow to more than 10 feet (3 m). Most carpet pythons seem to "bulk up" earlier in life than the allied diamond python, thus a healthy specimen of 10 feet (3 m) or more is a truly impressive snake. Make sure a snake of this size is legal in your community.

**Coloration:** Although varied in coloration, most are comparatively dull. The ground color may be yellow, cream, tan, or light-to-dark brown, over which are bands, spots, or stripes of darker brown or black. On some specimens, the dark color predominates; on other specimens, the reverse is true.

**Range:** Ranges throughout most of the Cape York Peninsula, Queensland, southward to northern New South Wales.

**Other subspecies:** Although several other subspecies of carpet pythons are recognized, all but the beautiful **"jungle" carpet python**, (*M. s. cheynei*) of northeastern Australia are uncommon in U.S. herpetoculture. The jungle carpet is the favorite of most U.S. herpetoculturists.

The color variability that we mentioned earlier pertains to the jungle carpet as much as the other races. Jungle carpets can vary from rather precisely delineated bands of bright yellow and black to an olive-tan ground color with broad, darker edged brown bands. Other phases include irregular but bright yellow bands against a black or brown ground, a pattern of yellow or cream bands or spots against a ground of black, and a series of light dorsal blotches or saddles either above or alternating with light lateral blotches. The light blotches of this latter may be regular or irregular and may be a rather bright yellow, but are usually cream to tan. Striped specimens have occasionally been found. In most cases, the stripes are better defined anteriorly than posteriorly. In addition to the stripes, the more typical blotches may, or may not, be present. Dark ocular stripes are always prominent. We had two large males that darkened with every shed until they were nearly monochromatic black.

The mere acquisition of a Tableland carpet does not necessarily assure that you will have one of the coveted yellow and black specimens. In most cases (but not always), brilliantly colored parents beget brilliantly colored progeny. Thus, knowing the color of the parent specimens will help you make an informed decision. If you are able to acquire a one- to two-year-old carpet python (when color changes have at least begun and patterns are well developed), you will have an even better idea of what it will look like as an adult.

The clutch size of the jungle carpet python varies considerably. The average is about 15 eggs, and the largest recorded number was 28.

The adult size of the Atherton Tableland carpet pythons is usually 6–8 feet (1.8–2.5 m).

The **northwestern carpet python** (*variegatus*) ranges eastward in coastal areas from the southwestern Cape York Peninsula to northern western Australia, and is apparently also the subspecies found in New Guinea. Attractively patterned with strongly contrasting, darker edged, irregular bands of brown, black, or red on a straw yellow ground, hatchlings are usually reddish but become less so with age. Attaining a length of about six feet (1.8 m), it is now readily available in U.S. herpetoculture.

Of the various subspecies, the yellow-specked black nominate form of forested eastern New South Wales, the beautiful **diamond python** (*M.s. spilota*), is the most difficult to obtain. We have also found it to be the most delicate of the subspecies, attaining an adult length of nearly seven feet (2.1 m).

**Intergrades:** Several races of the carpet python have now been interbred with the diamond python. Such crosses are well established in U.S. herpetoculture. These intergrades are beautiful snakes with immensely variable patterns and colors. Most look far more like their carpet than their diamond parent. Displaying what we often term "hybrid vigor," these intergrades are usually eager eaters and are often very easy to breed. Although it may not be necessary, we recommend the slight dropping of winter temperatures (70–72°F [21–22°C] night low, 78–82°F [26–28°C] day high), a

slight reduction in relative humidity, *and* the reduction of photoperiod.

Like the diamond and carpet pythons, the intergrade snakes breed in the winter, lay their eggs in early spring, and the 15 to 26 eggs hatch in late spring and early summer. The hatchlings are large and robust and readily accept rodents as their prey.

**Breeding:** In all of its many phases, forms, or morphs, the carpet python is both hardy and breeds readily with only a moderate winter cooling (especially ones from more tropical areas). Reduced photoperiod during the period of cooling is also important. Innumerable breeding successes have now made even the once seldom seen Atherton Tableland morphs readily available to those who want them. Prices range from about $100 for coastal Queensland carpet pythons of average appearance to $300 for the attractively colored Atherton Tableland phases.

**Morelia spilota cheneyi** *is referred to as the jungle carpet python by hobbyists. It often retains its brilliant color throughout its life.*

*This is a naturally occurring integrade between the Coastal carpet python,* **M. s. mcdowelli,** *and the diamond python,* **M. s. spilota.**

The coveted diamond–carpet python intergrades cost about $300.

The size, age, and health of the females and the subspecies involved determine the clutch size. We have had as few as 10 eggs from a small, young jungle carpet to more than 30 eggs from a large coastal carpet python.

As with most pythons, there are several ways to enhance your chances of breeding success with carpet pythons. The first way is to properly cycle your snakes. A winter regimen that will be perfectly fine for a tropical carpet python may not suffice for a carpet python that has originated from the more temperate southern extremes of the continent or for the diamond python. For more tropical pythons, a cooling during November and December to nighttime lows of 70–72°F (21–22°C) and daytime highs of 78–82°F (26–28°C) will suffice. It is either following or during their period of cooling that carpet pythons will usually begin their breeding sequences.

Except during periods of low barometric pressure (when they are sexually active at all times of day), most breeding activity seems to occur in the late afternoon or early evening. Once stimulated, breeding activities, including copulation, may continue throughout the night and well into the next day. Although, if properly cycled, they seldom need additional stimulation during periods of low barometric pressure (such as during the passage of a frontal system or at the advent of a severe thunderstorm). Gently misting the snakes may make them even more ardent. The misting can also be effective at other times. During stable weather, gently misting the cage once or twice in the late afternoon or early evening may activate your snakes.

The introduction of a new female or a second male to the cage of a cycled male may also provide breeding incentive. Do be advised, however, that the meeting of a second male carpet python by a sexually active snake can result in combat that can have devastating results (diamond pythons seem to not show overt aggression). Except for the breeding season, male snakes of all races may be either benign or only moderately agonistic toward each other. Supervise your specimens at all times and be ready to remove the nondominant male immediately if necessary. In many cases, the stimulation created when the second male is introduced will be immediate and will continue even after his removal. In addition, it is now known that introducing the recently shed skin of another male is nearly as effective a way to provide breeding stimulation, and it has none of the "worst-case possibilities."

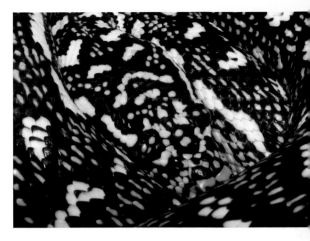

*A black ground color and well-defined white to yellow diamond-shaped spots typify the diamond python of Australia.*

Be particularly careful when handling (introducing, moving, removing) your male snakes at this time. Normally tractable snakes can become fully adversarial in only a moment.

The eggs of all of the subspecies of *M. spilota* are easily incubated, and the hatch ratio is usually excellent. One hundred percent hatches are not uncommon. Incubation temperatures between 88 and 92°F (31–33°C) seem best. High relative humidity should be maintained in the incubator. Although hatching usually occurs after about two months of incubation, eggs incubated at the higher temperatures hatch in less time than those maintained at lower temperatures. Embryo deformities and fatality may occur if eggs are incubated at temperatures above 92°F (33°C). For this reason, in relatively unsophisticated homestyle incubators which are subject to two or three-degree variations, we suggest a lower than maximum incubation temperature.

**Behavior:** Wild-collected specimens can be short tempered and untrustworthy, but will usually tame if handled gently and persistently. Once past the "snappy" hatchling stage (when all snakes are prone to bite the hand that handles or the hand that feeds), most captive bred carpet pythons are remarkably placid.

**Caging:** Despite their moderate to large adult size, diamond and carpet pythons are quite arboreal. This should be taken into account when providing housing for the snakes.

Carpet pythons are both hardy and attractive. They may be considered an excellent choice for either novice or advanced keepers.

# Green Tree Python, sp.
## Morelia viridis

**Coloration:** Although dull to bright green is the most common base color of adult green tree pythons (often referred to as "chondros" by hobbyists, a reference to an outmoded scientific name, *Chondropython viridis*), blue or yellow specimens are occasionally seen. An irregular and variable white vertebral stripe (or spots) is usually present. Blue markings are also often present on dorsal or lateral surfaces. Specimens originating from Aru Island are of a deeper green dorsal coloration and have powder-blue lips and venter.

Hatchlings are remarkably variable. Although most are brilliant yellow with a brown middorsal stripe and irregular brown flecking on the sides, some may be brick-red, russet, or chocolate brown. The brilliant juvenile coloration is soon replaced by the green of adulthood.

**Size:** Although occasionally attaining a seven-foot (2.1 m) length, most adults are six feet (1.8 m). Neonates are about one foot (31 cm) when emerging from the egg.

**Range:** This attractive python occurs widely in suitable habitats over much of New Guinea. It is also found on the Cape York Peninsula of northeastern Australia. Although far from helpless on the ground, green tree pythons are primarily arboreal. They are often seen coiled amid or atop clumps of epiphytic plants or lying quietly coiled while draped over a branch.

**Breeding:** Green tree pythons are an oviparous species. About one month after being successfully bred, ovulation occurs. It is from one to 15 months later that the female chondro lays her clutch of 10–25 eggs. Females incubate and protect their eggs. Incubation for fertile eggs usually lasts 56–63 days. A single clutch of eggs can produce hatchlings of several different colors, as mentioned earlier.

Although chondros have been bred by hobbyists for many years, they have remained one of the more problematic species. Egg death of the young after full-term development is common. Many hypotheses for this have been broached, but Trooper Walsh, believes that it is most likely due to a failure to reduce temperatures slightly during the final week of incubation. After years of monitoring the temperatures of maternally incubated eggs, Walsh has found that female chondros allow such a temperature fluctuation, with the first and final weeks being the cooler. Walsh especially stresses the importance of cooling the clutch on the tag end of the incubation period. A temperature regimen he has found most successful is: first week, 83°F (29.5°C); final week, 82°F (29°C); interim weeks, 89°F (32°C) days, with a slight drop to 86°F (30.5°C) nights. The relative humidity must always be high (95 percent or more), and good ventilation is a necessity. With this regimen, Walsh has established a 90 percent or better hatch rate.

Secure arboreal situations are chosen for the deposition site. In the wild, this site may be amid epiphytes or in a broad, secure crotch. In captivity cockatiel nesting boxes or an elevated wooden or plastic platform are accepted. As in the wild, a captive female will incubate her clutch if allowed. Incubation usually lasts less than two months.

**Caging:** Height and secure perches are more important to the well-being of green tree pythons than floor space. Tree limbs and a hide box affixed at or near the top of the cage offer the snakes the feeling of security that they need. Until fully acclimated, some chondros do not recognize a bowl as a drinking water source. They will, however, drink droplets of water from their coils if they are gently misted. Our breeders, kept outdoors for much of the

*Although still often called by its old generic name of Chondropython (chondro for short), the green tree python is now known scientifically as **Morelia viridis**.*

*Varying by populations, hatchling green tree pythons are yellow, orange, or burgundy. A few adults, such as this "canary chondro" retain the brilliant juvenile color throughout their lives.*

**Comments:** This beautiful snake is still often referred to by its older name of *C. viridis*. Like many arboreal snakes, chondros are laterally compressed and have a strongly prehensile tail. They are wait-and-ambush feeders and often constrict their prey while hanging from a branch, supported solely by their tail. Small rodents, lizards, and frogs are accepted by the hatchlings. Adults seem to prefer suitably sized mammals and birds, but will accept lizards as well. Because their "prey-capture instinct" is stimulated by movement, hatchling chondros often ignore quiescent "pinky" mice. The little snakes are much more apt to accept older mice ("jumpers") that are moving quickly about.

Although we have always considered chondros a "just look, don't touch" kind of snake, others may enjoy handling their snakes. Green tree pythons vary tremendously in temperament. Some are defensive and irascible, whereas others are relatively quiet and approachable. Most are somewhere between these two extremes, being approachable at times but striking and biting at other times. It is usually possible to handle safely even the worst-tempered green tree python by manipulating it gently with a snake hook. From the hook the snake can be placed on a limb or other inanimate perch, where it will coil and often stay (unless moved again) for long periods of time.

year, were most active during the atmospheric pressure drops that were associated with our frequent thunderstorms. At that time, they would feed, prowl, drink, and defecate. Misting the snakes from above with a hose would also activate them, but not to the extent of a natural storm. Interestingly, many herpetoculturists believe that the low pressures typically associated with storm systems stimulate chondros to breed, even when they are in indoor cages.

# Burmese Python
## *Python molurus bivittatus*

**Comments and cautions:** The most commonly seen and often bred large python in the world, this nonendangered race of the endangered Indian python is illegal in many states. Known for its fecundity and its calm and placid disposition, it is the *wrong* choice for most hobbyists because of its adult size. This snake will grow to be more than 10 feet (3 m) in length within the first three years. A python this large can easily kill its human keeper, or a child, and some have done so. In most cases it is a misdirected feeding response that has led to the disaster, but regardless of the reason, you can be seriously hurt. It is illegal to release any non-mature snake (or other animal) into the wild.

We urge you to read the following species account carefully and to assess and reassess the wisdom of acquiring a giant constrictor. These big snakes are *not* for the casual hobbyist. There are caging and handling precautions you must take that you wouldn't need with a smaller snake. It is very important that when it's a baby you feed your python in a box, separate from its "home" tank. This way, the snake will learn to associate the feeding box, not its keeper, with the introduction of food. After handling a food animal, *before* handling your python, carefully wash the scent of the prey from your hands and arms and change clothes, if necessary. If you smell like food, your snake will treat you like food. Snakes act and react primarily on instinct, not intelligent assessment. Do not attribute to your python a power of discernment of which it is incapable.

**Coloration:** The normal color of the Burmese python consists of a tan to brown ground with dark-edged olive-brown dorsal and lateral blotches. A well-defined dark spearhead is present on the top of the head.

**Variants:** Many colors and patterns have been selectively bred and are now readily available. One is the **"green"** or **"patternless"** Burmese. Both names can be deceptive. The green merely means an overall olive-brown shade. As babies, most of these snakes have a reduced, but still strongly evident, pattern. The pattern does become obscured with age and may be entirely obliterated by the time the snake attains a length of four or five feet (1.2–1.5 m). This phase is also available as an albino (the **albino green** Burmese).

A pale brown phase, called the **cinnamon** Burmese, has been developed. In the normal phase, the basic brown tones are paler than a normal Burmese. The ground color actually nears cinnamon. Both an **albino cinnamon** and a **green cinnamon** are available.

A fragmented pattern anomaly is called the **"labyrinth"** Burmese. This fragmentation has been further broken into a new morph called the **granite** phase.

**Size:** An 18-inch (46 cm) long hatchling can reach eight feet (2.5 m) in length in only one to two years! The growth may then slow somewhat, but Burmese pythons usually reach a length of 12–14 feet (3.7–4.3 m), a housing challenge for even the most dedicated snake keeper. Sexual maturity is reached at a length of 7–10 feet (2.1–3 m). Burmese pythons are heavy bodied, and females tend to get much larger than males.

**Range:** In addition to Burma, they are found in Indonesia and Malaysia and may live in a variety of habitats, ranging from open fields and farmland to woodlands and forests. Introduced to Florida.

**Caging:** While a baby will comfortably reside in a 10-gallon (38 L) tank, a 4–6 foot yearling will require a 55-gallon (208 L) tank, and an eight-foot (2.5 m) two-year-old specimen should have about a 100-gallon (380 L) tank. You will probably feel comfortable housing a 10-foot (3 m) python in a 100-gallon (380 L) tank, but a 12–15-foot (3.7–4.6 m) python requires a cage with a floor space of about 4 × 8 feet (1.2 × 2.5 m). When the snake exceeds 15 feet (4.6 m), many hobbyists actually remodel and dedicate a suitably heated room to the serpents, especially if housing more than a single snake.

**Feeding:** In addition to the challenges of adequate caging are the challenges of *feed-*

*ing* the snake. Few people object to feeding a hatchling the required amount of adult mice, and most keepers don't even object to feeding the yearling python the number of rats it will need. Some keepers, however, are squeamish about feeding the python the guinea pigs, chicks, ducks, and rabbits that it will require as a young to fully grown adult.

**Breeding:** In keeping with its large size, the Burmese python has large clutches of large eggs. Average-sized females often have 30–40 eggs, and very large specimens sometimes lay more than 60 eggs. This is why released Burmese are a big problem in the Everglades. Incubation temperatures of 85–88°F (229–31°C) should be maintained, and the relative humidity should be high, but not saturated. Females will readily incubate their own eggs if allowed. During maternal incubation, the female wraps around her clutch and actually elevates her body temperature to a more suitable level by initiating a series of shiver-like muscle contractions. Some females may defend their clutches, striking repeatedly as you attempt to remove the eggs for incubation; others will remain relatively benign. (See page 31 for suggested incubation techniques.)

The reticulated python, *Python recticulatus*, is a big, often bad-tempered, python native to Asia but which is now captive-bred in large numbers. We do not recommend it as a pet because of its habit of determined slashing, biting, and untrustworthiness.

*Now available in many colors and patterns (this is an albino), Burmese pythons, **Python molurus bivittatus**, may quickly grow to more than 10 feet (3 m) long and are illegal to keep in many areas.*

# COLUBRINE SNAKES

*Most colubrines are very hardy, and some are extremely colorful. Thus they are often thought of as excellent snakes for both beginning and advanced hobbyists.*

The vast family of colubrine snakes (family Colubridae) contains more than 1,500 species collectively referred to as "harmless snakes." This is a misnomer, for many colubrine species have enlarged teeth at the rear of the upper jaw or venoms of varying toxicity.

We discuss none of the truly rear-fanged snakes in this section, but we do mention the hog-nosed snakes (members of the subfamily Xenodontinae), which have a large number of devotees, with enlarged teeth and a questionable toxicity. The rat, king, gopher, indigo, house, and green snakes are members of the subfamily Colubrinae. The garter and water snakes and their allies are members of the subfamily Natricinae, a bite from which can cause variable adverse reactions.

The colubrines employ numerous feeding strategies. The rat, king, gopher, and house snakes either trail or ambush their prey, which is then killed by constriction. Indigos swallow their prey alive, often immobilizing large prey items by throwing a loose coil over and pinning it to the ground. Garter, water, brown, and green snakes eat their worm, fish, slug, and insect prey alive. Hog-nosed snakes can be messy eaters, puncturing and bloodying inflated toads with their long rear teeth.

The dispositions and handleability of colubrines varies both by species and by individual. Although American corn and rat snakes and European rat snakes may bite, they usually rapidly become tractable if gently handled. Asiatic rat snakes may be persistently feisty. Frightened garter snakes may bite and smear musk or feces when restrained. Kingsnakes may coil quietly around a hand or arm, and then seize and chew that hand animatedly. Milksnakes tend to be squirmy, to occasionally bite, and may never become entirely at ease when being handled. African house snakes are usually relatively placid. Until they are used to handling, the tropical indigo snakes may strike and bite savagely. If frightened, hog-nosed snakes hood, writhe, and if additionally stressed, roll upside down and play dead. Green snakes may writhe and gape, but almost never bite or smear cloacal contents.

*This Colubrine is an Everglades rat snake, Pantherophis obsoletus rossalleni.*

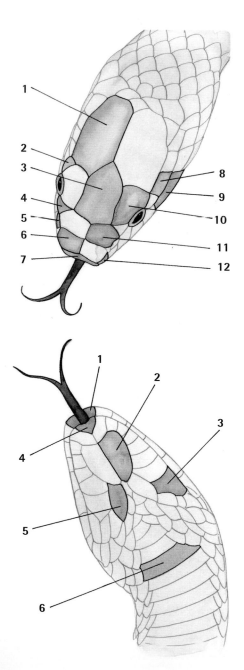

*Dorsal view of scales on the top of the head.*

1. Parietal
2. Postocular
3. Frontal
4. Preocular
5. Loreal
6. Internasal

7. Rostral
8. Temporal
9. Upper labial
10. Supraocular
11. Prefrontal
12. Nasal

The two snake species most eagerly sought for pets are the corn snake and the California kingsnake. Both are now available in many mutant colorations and patterns, and most specimens available are the result of captive breedings. Other species of rat, milk, and king-snakes are also immensely popular with hobbyists. The various house snakes are cyclic in popularity, but seem destined for greater hobbyist acceptance. Garter, ribbon, brown, and green snakes are backyard species that are often taken captive when found and are often the first species kept by young enthusiasts. Some garter snakes (including color mutations) are bred in large numbers for pet markets.

The various colubrines vary from less than one foot (30 cm) in length (brown snakes) to

*Ventral view of scales on the bottom or chin of a snake.*

1. Rostral
2. Anterior chin shield
3. Lower labial

4. Mental
5. Posterior chin shield
6. Ventral

*While the head scales of some snakes are fragmented and difficult to identify, the large head scales of most species of harmless snakes are designated here.*

*Adult Baird's rat snakes bear four dark stripes, with those from southern Mexico being the most intensely orange.*

more than eight feet (2.5 m) (Neotropical indigos). For discussions of some other colubrines, please see Barron's *Corn and Other Rat Snakes* (Bartlett and Bartlett) and *Kingsnakes and Milksnakes* (Markel and Bartlett).

# Corn and Other American Rat Snakes

There are six species of New World rat snakes of the genus *Pantherophis* and all calm down and eat well in captivity. We will discuss only four—the Baird's rat snake; the corn snake and its western subspecies; the Great Plains rat snake; and the black rat snake and its subspecies. These may occasionally be found in barns, deserted buildings, roadside dumps, or under other human debris. The eastern species are arboreal and primarily nocturnal.

As their name indicates, these snakes feed primarily on rodents. Their origin in temperate areas of North America indicates that they won't need a lot of temperature control to do well in captivity. Specimens from colder climes may need hibernation to cycle reproductively; those from the deep south require, if anything, little more than photoperiod manipulation. Snakes from many generations of captive breeding are easier to breed and cycle than wild-collected specimens.

## Baird's Rat Snake
### *Pantherophis bairdi*

Baird's rat snake is a subtly colored species that is just now gaining in popularity with American hobbyists. Dorsally, adults range from a pearl gray to a dusty orange-brown to a burnt orange. Adult snakes have four dark to orangish stripes, with the stripes on the back usually being more distinct than those on the sides. The interstitial skin and even the leading edge of each scale may be a bright orange. The venter is usually an unpatterned yellow to orange. The most intensely orange snakes seem to come from the southernmost part of the Mexican states of Nuevo Leon and Tamaulipas.

Hatchlings and juveniles are grayish with a busy pattern of thin dorsal saddles and well-defined lateral blotches. A curved dark bar crosses the snout immediately anterior to the eyes, and a dark diagonal postocular stripe runs from eye to mouth. With maturity, both markings pale and disappear. The head of an adult Baird's rat snake has no markings.

**Size:** A moderately heavy-bodied snake with a maximum size just over five feet (15 m), the females are generally longer.

**Range:** Southward from central Texas, in disjunct areas, to northeastern Mexico.

**Reproduction:** Although they reproduce best if hibernated, our pairs produced viable eggs with little more than a slight winter cooling and a reduction of photoperiod. Hatchlings

*A pretty Miami phase corn snake.*

are about a foot (31 cm) in length. Clutches number from 4–10 eggs. Hatching occurs after 2½ months at an incubation temperature of 82°–86°F (28–29°C). Hatchlings almost always feed readily on newborn mice. Large, healthy females can produce two clutches annually.

**Comments:** Both the Mexican and Texas color morphs are now being bred by hobbyists. The Mexican differs from the Texas specimens by a gray head and a ground color suffused with orange. With captive breeding, these once rather expensive snakes are now being seen with increasing frequency—and at decreasing prices.

Baird's rat snake (named after Spencer Fullerton Baird, a 19th-century vertebrate zoologist), originally considered a subspecies of *obsoleta*, is attractive, easily handled, and very hardy.

## Corn Snake
*P. guttata guttata*

Few hobbyists need any introduction to the corn snake. Medium-sized (six feet [1.8 m] for a large specimen) with red-on-gray or red-on-orange blotches, this southeastern U.S. snake is probably the most popular, having been bred in captivity for more than 40 years.

Decades of breeding programs have added more than 20 colors and patterns to the normal blotched phase. However, many hobbyists think nothing is more attractive than the common, normal, corn snake.

There's a lot of color variety in the term "normal," which we consider to be any color phase occurring in the wild in sufficient numbers as to form a viable, sustainable population. The Okeetee, Miami, and Hastings phase corn snakes are "normals," as are the dark anerythristic corn snakes from southwest Florida and the rosy rat snakes from the Florida Keys. The blood red phase and albino corn phase have also been found in the wild, but not in sufficient numbers to constitute a population.

**Okeetee phase** corn snakes are noted for their brilliance. Bright scarlet saddles, broadly edged with black and set against a red-orange ground color is the naturally occurring color phase in eastern Georgia and South and North Carolina. Beyond (and even within) this region, colors may vary and be less intense.

**Anerythristic:** Despite rampant and habitat modifying development, southwest Florida remains a popular location for anerythristic corn snakes (ones that lack red pigment). This color phase, also called "black albino" and "melanistic" by hobbyists, has black or deep brown saddles on a gray background and often has a yellow or peach wash on the sides of the neck. However, except for the black "corn snake spearpoint" on the head, the snake is more reminiscent of a black rat snake.

**Blood red:** Morphs originally found among normally colored individuals in northeastern Florida, their name refers to their deep red coloration. Sadly, the hatchlings are among the most difficult to induce to feed. Even once started, not all thrive. Problems have continued, even with outbreeding followed by a subsequent redevelopment of the red strain. If you are considering this morph, watch it feed before you buy it.

**Miami phase:** Although very different and less lauded than the coveted Okeetee phase, the Miami phase corn snake is also beautiful and hardy. Its "maroon on pearl-gray or silver" coloration is a familiar sight over much of the southern third of the Florida peninsula. This amazingly resilient snake persists even amidst the rubble-surrounded warehouse complexes of downtown Miami.

**Rosy rat snake:** This term is a hobbyist's designation for the small, faded corn snakes of the Florida Keys. Once thought to be a standardized pale rose on rose color with a little black in the patterning, we now realize Rosies come in a variety of hues. Rosies may be orange (rosy ground color with orange blotches), olive (olive-drab ground with an army blanket green wash on the head and orange blotches), silver (gray to gun-metal blue ground with red-orange blotches), and chocolate (brownish ground with orange blotches). Many of these phases have been refined and perpetuated by John Decker, a rosy rat snake specialist breeder in Hollywood, Florida. (For those who wish to collect their own specimens, be aware that the corn snakes of the lower Florida Keys are now protected by Florida law.)

**Designer corn snakes:** The following names all refer to herpetoculturally derived color phases of the corn snake: Sunglow, amelansitic Okeetee, candycane, snow, ghost, blizzard, Christmas, caramel, mocha, and butter. Names

*This is a brightly colored corn snake from Hendry County, Florida.*

The corn snakes from the Florida Keys
may have a ground color of rosy-red, olive
(pictured here), or silver-gray. They were
originally referred to as "rosy rat snakes."

such as zigzag or zipper, motley or mottled, and striped, refer to pattern anomalies. The name "creamsicle" has been coined for the beautiful amelanistic cross between the corn and the Great Plains rat snake. A beautiful yellow-white snake with peach to pale-orange blotches, its color intensifies with age.

*Despite its plain coloration, the Great Plains rat snake has given rise to some spectacular color morphs.*

### Great Plains Rat Snake
### *P. guttata emoryi*

The Great Plains rat snake is currently considered a subspecies of the corn snake by some authorities and a full species by others. It looks much like a corn snake but with dark gray saddles on a gray-to-olive-gray background.

**Size:** The Great Plains rat snake seldom exceeds 4.5 feet (1.4 m) in length, and the record length is only 5¼ feet (1.6 m).

**Range:** It is common in our central states and in northeastern Mexico.

**Reproduction:** Because most Great Plains rat snakes originate from cooler areas than corn snakes, a period of actual hibernation may be required to cycle them for breeding. A reduction in winter temperature (to 45–52°F [7–11°C]) and photoperiod for 70 to 90 days is recommended.

Because they are so outshone by the more easterly corn snake, not many hobbyists seek out the Great Plains rat snake, and is less popular in captive-breeding programs. However, through intergrading the Great Plains rat snake and the corn snake, the spectacular "creamsicle corn" was developed. Although wild albino Great Plains rat snakes have been found, most seen in captivity have albino corn snake genes in their background.

**Food:** The adult corn snake and the Great Plains rat snake feed primarily on rodents, but the diet in the wild (especially for the younger

snakes) includes bats, birds, lizards, and frogs. The prey is killed by constriction.

## Black Rat Snake
### *P. o. obsoletus*

Though of a dark color and less visually appealing than some of its other subspecies, many new reptile enthusiasts like this snake.

**Coloration:** The normal coloration varies. The darkest (blackest) individuals seem to come from the northeast and the mountains of the southeast. Specimens in the southern Blue Ridge Mountains have been as dark as specimens in the Berkshires of Massachusetts. Black rat snakes from the western part of the range are often more brown than black. The largest tend to be the darkest. Under bright lighting, the dark blotches of babyhood are still usually seen. The light ground color becomes suffused with melanin, finally obscuring the dorsal blotching. The interstitial skin may be lighter, being white or reddish, and the throat is light (often white). The chin coloration may extend for a variable distance onto the venter.

**Variants:** At least two genetically distinct albino forms are available, plus albino intergrades between black rat snakes and other races are now available to hobbyists under names which may—or may not—reflect their lineage.

A brindle black rat snake has been developed as well as a "bubblegum" variant, an albino

hybrid between Everglades, yellow, and black rat snakes.

**Size:** Largest of the several subspecies and with a record size of 101 inches (2.5 m).

**Range:** It ranges from the southern tip of Ontario, southern Massachusetts, and southeastern Minnesota, southward to northern

*This black rat snake,* **Pantherophis o. obsoletus,** *is from Kansas.*

Louisiana and central Georgia. It is not usually found in the coastal plain of the Carolinas where it is replaced by the smaller but the more brightly colored yellow rat snake.

**Breeding:** These snakes do well either with or without a period of winter dormancy; although those from northern areas seem to need winter dormancy for reproduction. Most feed readily year-round if kept warm. Captive-breeding supplies most of the specimens available in the pet market. All the obsoletus are oviparous, and most can attain sexual maturity in their second summer. Small and young specimens have fewer and smaller eggs. The clutch of an old, healthy female (from three years of age and up) often contains 25 or more eggs. The eggs are easily incubated and hatched, and the hatchling snakes are robust and easily reared. Hatchlings have dark saddles on a deep-gray (gray rat snake) to pinkish (Everglades rat snake) ground color and can exceed 1 foot (31 cm) in length; some of 16 inches (41 cm) in length have been reported.

**Subspecies:** Of its very well-known subspecies, perhaps the best known is the yellow rat snake (*P. o. quadrivittatus*).

## Yellow Rat Snake
### *P. o. quadrivittatus*

The adult has a variably yellow or yellow-green ground color. Most have four prominent dark lines. All have a distinct odor and their musk is strongly pungent. This subspecies ranges southward along the coastal plain from just south of North Carolina's Albemarle Peninsula to the central Florida Keys.

The most intensely colored specimens **Deckert's** or **Keys rat snakes** occur from the southern tip of Florida to Pine Key. This variant retains the juvenile saddles throughout its life, but also develops stripes with age. The ground color may be yellow-orange, deep orange, or brownish-orange, and the tongue is black. The saddles can be prominent or vague and of a brownish to maroon color. The most attractive animals are those with the deep orange ground color and maroon saddles. Apparently this snake has never been common. Today, a Keys variant yellow rat snake is considered much harder to find than the "rosy rat" corn snake.

**Albino yellow rat snakes** have been collected and are being bred. They retain the saddles but the stripes are poorly defined.

**Intergrades:** The **"greenish rat snake"** is a naturally occurring intergrade between the yellow and the black rat snakes. It is common where the ranges of the two subspecies abut in areas of Georgia, extreme southern South

*Depending on the locale from which they come, yellow rat snakes,* **Pantherophis obsoletus quadrivittatus,** *may have either very dark stripes on a yellow background (such as this example from northern Florida) or paler stripes on an orange background.*

Carolina, and on northward to southeastern Tennessee. Often of a dingy olive color when adult, the four stripes are usually prominent.

The **Gulf Hammock rat snake** of northwestern peninsular Florida is also a naturally occurring intergrade between the gray rat and the yellow rat snakes. Of grayish ground color, this snake retains the juvenile saddles and develops the usual yellow rat four stripes.

## Everglades Rat Snake
### Pantherophis obsoletus rossalleni

Today, because of habitat modifications resulting from the extensive draining of Florida's Everglades, the beautiful Everglades rat snake—that apparently evolved amidst and was adapted to the once-flooded sawgrass prairies—is now seldom seen in its phenotypically pure form. That a precious few do remain in the vicinity of Lake Okeechobee is ascertained by the occasional finding of one amidst the hordes of yellow rat snakes that have, with the draining, invaded the region and genetically outcompeted their orange relatives.

This very hardy, easily kept, five-to-six-foot (1.5–1.8 m) long snake (hatchlings are about 10 inches (25 cm) long and of very different appearance than the adults) was described in 1949 by Florida herpetologist Wilfred T. Neill. His description follows (the accents are ours): "ground color of adults *rich orange, orange-yellow*, or *orange-brown*; dorsal and lateral stripes present but not sharply defined, of a dull gray-brown shade; a vague sublateral

*The beautiful Everglades rat snake, Pantherophis obsoletus rossalleni, is found in diminishing numbers near Lake Okeechobee, Florida.*

*This albino yellow rat snake was found near Lake Okeechobee in southern Florida.*

stripe, evident posteriorly on the tips of the ventrals; *chin and throat bright orange; venter bright orange or orange-yellow*; scales with a glaucous sheen, at least anteriorly; iris orange; *tongue bright red*. The diagnostic coloration is assumed at an early age..." A mustard yellow chin with either a yellow or a white mental groove (the longitudinal groove in the center of the chin) is also acceptable.

We have been loosely monitoring the declining populations of the Everglades rat snake

*Hatchlings of the Everglades rat snake tend to be paler and pinker than the hatchlings of other subspecies.*

since the 1960s. With each passing decade they have become harder to find, but in their now well-drained habitat, yellow rat snakes (a subspecies that evolved in much drier conditions) have become far more common. Nor are Everglades rat snakes having the correct phenotype any easier to find in herpetocultural circles. Stated simply, although you may see a rat snake of correct dorsal and ventral color-

ation, unless the secondary characteristics—the throat, chin, and tongue—are also of the correct color, the snake is not a pure Everglades.

## Gray Rat Snake
### P. o. spiloides

The deep south's lighter-colored version of the north's black rat snake actually has two color phases: the rather dark, gray-on-gray **"normal phase"** and the lighter, more attractive gray on grayish-white **"white-oak phase."** The dark dorsal saddles (which this subspecies retains throughout its life) are often bordered with an even darker, narrow edging; those of the white oak phase are often narrowly edged with a very light gray. The saddles may be completely dark or light centered. The biggest recorded gray rat was 84.25 inches (214 m). Gray rat snakes may be encountered from coastal panhandle Florida to western Missouri, ranging northward to northern Alabama and in the somewhat warmer Mississippi River valley to extreme western Kentucky, southeastern Illinois, and immediately adjacent Indiana.

## Texas Rat Snake
### P. o. lindheimerii

Named for herpetologist Fred Lindheimer, its distinguishing characteristic is its belligerence. We know of no other nonvenomous snake in the U.S. that so readily bites, or that strikes so many times in rapid succession. Plus, this is not an attractive snake. It retains its blotches throughout its life, and it's lighter than a black rat and darker than a gray rat. The ground

*Gray rat snakes,* **Pantherophis obsoletus spiloides,** *are interesting but are not greatly favored by hobbyists.*

*You may think the Texas rat snake attractive, but most hobbyists get tired of being bitten every time they hold this snake.*

color can vary from straw-yellow to orange, but usually it is tan or light brown. The dorsal blotches are rather elongate, fairly narrow, and medium to deep brown, with or without light centers. The contrast between the dark dorsal blotches and the lighter ground color is not very great. The lateral interstitial skin can vary from yellow to orange. The interstitial color may spill over onto the leading edges of some lateral scales, but since the trailing edge of the preceding scales overlaps, the little brilliance may not be seen unless the snake is distended with food or tightly coiled.

**Other morphs:** Few hobbyists work with normal, wild-caught Texas rat snakes, but many keep and breed two of the most common mutants—an albino (actually amelanistic rather than a true albino) and a leucistic. The albino is the less attractive, being white (almost translucent when hatched) with pink saddles and pink eyes. The colors intensify somewhat with increasing age. The dorsal saddles of older adults are usually pale strawberry. The leucistic morph is beautiful, with a solid, unpatterned white and gray-blue eyes.

# Kingsnakes and Milksnakes

Although they are quite closely allied to the rat and the gopher snakes, milksnakes and kingsnakes are very different in appearance and actions. Milksnakes and kingsnakes are more secretive, usually have heads only slightly larger than their neck, are quite cannibalistic, and many are resistant to the venoms of pit vipers.

Babies are more prone to cannibalism; you should house and especially feed milksnakes and kingsnakes of all sizes separately.

Besides other snakes, in the wild, milksnakes and kingsnakes eat amphibians, lizards and their eggs, hatchling turtles and turtle eggs, and suitably sized rodents. Most captives will adapt well to a diet exclusively of lab rodents.

Milksnakes are one of the most brightly colored snakes, clad in rings of red, black, and yellow (or white). Gaudy when seen in a cage, when moving in the wild they blend in with backgrounds surprisingly well. When encountered in the wild, milksnakes and kingsnakes may draw their necks into an "S" and strike animatedly. Despite this initial show of bravado, kingsnakes usually quiet down and become less belligerent after only a few handlings, but most milksnakes remain nervous and may resent handling throughout their lives. Despite this, their beauty endears them to hobbyists, and they are eagerly sought.

Although we don't consider these snakes as satisfying captives as rat and gopher snakes, brisk sales at reptile shows and pet shops show that many hobbyists think otherwise.

## Common Kingsnake
*Lampropeltis getula* ssp.

**Eastern kingsnake,** *Lampropeltis g. getula*:
Because of the chain-like pattern of white or cream markings against the shiny black or deep brown ground color, the large (up to 82 inches [2.1 m]), robust, nominate form is often referred to as the "chain king." Found in suitable habitats from central New Jersey southward to northern Florida and westward to the Appalachians and southeastern Alabama, it tames readily in captivity and feeds well on rodents.

*The eastern kingsnake,* Lampropeltis g. getula, *has always been popular.*

Adult females lay from 6–12 eggs. Except for the red on their flanks, hatchlings are diminutive replicas of the adults. They are hardy, feed easily, and grow rapidly. There are albino forms.

Hatchlings may have a considerable amount of strawberry red or russet along their flanks.

**California kingsnake,** *L. g. californiae*: This moderately sized (3.5–4.25 feet [1.1–1.3 m]) snake is, to kingsnake breeders, what the corn snake is to rat snake breeders. They make good pets once they adjust to captivity. Although naturally somewhat variable, "Cal kings," as they are called by hobbyists, are now available in many hues and patterns Mother Nature never imagined. Albinos may be more commonly seen than "normally" colored specimens, which are banded in white or cream against a black or deep-brown ground. The bands may continue around the belly, or the belly may be primarily dark or light. The stark black and white specimens are often referred to as the "desert phase" and were once thought to represent a separate, now unrecognized, subspecies—*yumensis*.

Like all kingsnakes, the Cal king is a powerful constrictor and an opportunistic feeder. It will eat amphibians, reptiles (including baby turtles and snakes), small ground-nesting birds, and small mammals. Captives feed on lab mice.

*A "high yellow" striped Cal king. Until captive breeding revealed that color variants could occur in the same clutch of eggs, hobbyists went crazy trying to figure out regional distributions of Cal king "races."*

*Immensely variable, the California kingsnake,* Lampropeltis getula californiae, *may be striped, banded, barred, or blotched, and have a ground color of black or brown.*

**Breeding:** Well-fed Cal kings grow rapidly and may be large and old enough to breed in their second year of life, and definitely by their third year. Males, which grow more slowly than the females, can breed successfully at a younger age. After having been captive-bred for several generations, the "domestic" offspring are easier to cycle reproductively than wild-collected specimens. After having reached sexual maturity, our captive-produced Cal kings have cycled and produced large clutches of viable eggs with no more preparation than a natural photoperiod and a good body weight. Large, healthy females may produce a second clutch of eggs. But we have not successfully bred wild-collected specimens without hibernating them.

**Variants:** In addition to the desert phase and the normal ones, other herpetocultural variants include:

**1.** 50/50: Dark and light colorations are of nearly equal extent with a variable pattern that usually combines partial striping with banding. A banana (or high yellow) of enhanced brilliance has also been developed.

**2.** The striped pattern, rather uncommon in nature, has been perpetuated by captive-breeding programs.

**3.** The southern Baja Peninsula is home to a California kingsnake with a poorly defined,

*The Apalachicola Lowlands kingsnake,* Lampropeltis getula *ssp., has a small range near the Apalachicola River on Florida's panhandle.*

*very* narrow, often cinnamon vertebral stripe. Once known as *L. g. nitida*, it is still referred to as the South Baja "*nitida*" phase by hobbyists. Further north on the peninsula we encounter the mid-Baja "conjuncta" phase, which has very narrow, poorly defined light banding. On some dark specimens, in subdued lighting, the banding may be barely discernible. A rather similar-appearing animal, usually called "melanistic" by hobbyists, is found in mid-California.

**Some natural Florida intergrades:** Because taxonomists and hobbyists interpret the concept of "species" and "subspecies" differently, the views of the two often differ sharply. This is the case with the **"Apalachicola Lowland"**

(blotched) kingsnake (*L. g. getula* x *L. g. floridana*). To hobbyists, this tremendously variable form will always be the "blotched" kingsnake, *L. getula* ssp. The exact genetics of this attractive and variable kingsnake remain conjectural and will stay so until studies, currently underway, are completed. Found in Gulf and Calhoun Counties, Florida, the blotched form is only one color and pattern extreme of a very variable kingsnake. In fact, this coveted snake of the northern Florida hinterlands displays nearly as much variation as the better known California kingsnake. However, when a vertebral stripe is present, it is dark rather than light.

Large and robust, captives have grown to six feet (1.8 m) in length, exceeding the longest recorded wild specimen by more than four inches (10 cm). Hatchlings are usually darker or redder than the adults. They feed readily and grow rapidly. Normal clutch size is 6–12 eggs.

*A classic example of the Florida kingsnake (formerly known as the Brook's kingsnake) is a beautiful serpent.*

The **Peninsula intergrade kingsnake**, another intergradation between *L. g. floridana* and *L. g. getula*, was once known as the Florida kingsnake and is still called this by most breeders and pet trade operators. Hardy and prolific, it feeds well, grows rapidly, quiets quickly, and breeds readily. These interesting snakes have a light to dark brown ground coloration with numerous (22–66) cream to yellow crossbands. Light spots on the dark body scales can impart a vaguely speckled appearance. Hatchlings may have considerable red on the flanks but are otherwise similar to adults. This is one of the few kingsnakes in which the wild-collected specimens still seem to outnumber the captive bred and born hatchlings in the pet trade.

Intergrade kingsnakes may occasionally exceed five feet (1.5 m) in length.

**Florida kingsnake**, *L. g. floridana*: This race is confusing to many hobbyists. Variably colored, but often quite yellow, they were once called *L. g. brooksi*. Dealers and hobbyists are still likely to call them "Brook's kingsnakes." These pale snakes of the oolitic limestone prairies of extreme south Florida are coveted by hobbyists, avidly sought by herpetoculturists, and bring the highest prices to breeders. Brook's are not really rare in the wild. What are rare are the very palest morphs, so eagerly sought by hobbyists and found ONLY on the high and dry, exposed, pock-marked, white oolitic limestone outcroppings. Specimens found virtually next to them in the mucklands of the southern Everglades are considerably darker. Even in the choicest habitat, color variation is apparent.

The Florida kingsnake, as now understood, is somewhat smaller than its conspecifics from further north. A length of four feet (1.2 m) is commonly attained and Conant/Collins report a 69.5-inch (1.77 m) record size. Males are a bit larger and of lighter color.

Clutch size ranges from 4–12, and the robust hatchlings are much darker than the adults. Like many of the eastern kingsnakes, hatchlings may have considerable red on the sides. This fades to the adult coloration after a few sheds.

Several other subspecies of the eastern king-snake are available in the pet trade but not as popular. The black king, *L. g. nigra*, of the highlands of the southeastern United States is perhaps the least popular. It is similar to, but darker than, the speckled kingsnake, *L. g. holbrooki* of the Mississippi Valley and associated drainages. Both are prone to unpleasant dispositions and are more predisposed to cannibalism. The desert king, *L. g. splendida*, is the most attractive of these several forms. It is a species of the Chihuahuan desert of the U.S. and northern Mexico. The Mexican black king, *L. g. nigritus*, may be vaguely patterned or jet black. It is of fairly placid disposition and, because of the many similarities between it and the California kingsnake, a fair amount of interest is shown by hobbyists.

**Comments:** Although in the east and in other normally moist regions kingsnakes may be encountered some distance from water, in more arid areas they are associated with swamp, marsh, or riveredge habitats. In addition to the foods mentioned here, these powerful constrictors will overpower and consume native venomous snake species. Despite this, kingsnakes are not the dedicated enemies of venomous snakes as many people think.

*This pure white albino Honduran milksnake was produced by Terry Dunham.*

## Milk and Scarlet Kingsnakes
### *L. triangulum* ssp.

No snake book would be complete without mention of these remarkably beautiful, hardy, and popular snakes. This section will give you only an idea of the variety in this group. (For more information see *Kingsnakes and Milksnakes: A Complete Pet Care Manual* by Markel and Bartlett.) The only disadvantage of having these snakes is their slight nervousness and their need for privacy and seclusion.

The very variable **Honduran milksnake**, *L. t. hondurensis*, is one of the most popular of the tropical American forms. It occurs in a typical black, yellow, and red-ringed milk snake form

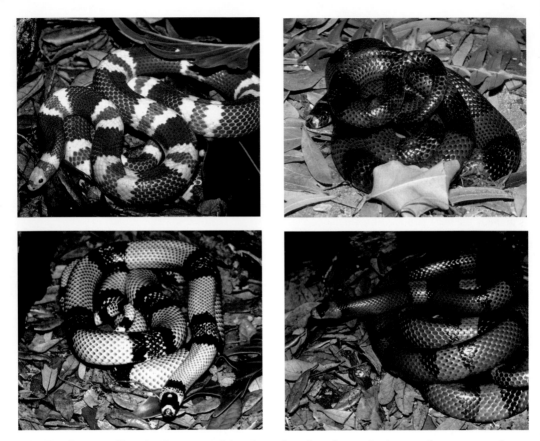

*The Honduran milksnake,* Lampropeltis triangulum hondurensis, *is now the most popular of the milksnakes. More than a dozen color and pattern phases are available.*

as well as a startling red-orange, black and orange-banded "tangerine" form. Albinos are now available to hobbyists but are expensive.

Adult *hondurensis* generally exceed a fairly heavy 3.5 feet (1.1 m) in total length; a very few may grow to 5 feet (1.5 m). Healthy hatchlings can exceed 15 inches (38 cm) in length, and usually feed readily on pinky mice.

**Caging:** Like all milksnakes (all members of the genus, in fact), Honduran milks are secre-tive snakes. They ably find their way beneath surface debris, both of natural and manmade origin, and are fully capable of making their own tunnels in loose soils. They are very good escape artists, and their constant nudging habits enable them to find the weakest point of caging. Cage them *securely!*

A thick substrate of cypress mulch, aspen shavings, or fallen leaves ensures that the snakes will feel secure, but negates easy viewing of the snakes. Because of this, milksnakes of all kinds are less satisfactory pet snakes than many snakes of other genera. However, if you can enjoy them under conditions when they feel secure, they make very suitable pets.

Hiding boxes and furniture of fallen limbs or secured rocks will also be appreciated by the snakes. By keeping them on a substrate of newspaper with a hide box or two, you can control where they are in their cage, and you need only to lift the hide box to see them.

Fresh water in a low but fairly large dish is mandatory. Milksnakes will often soak in their water for a day or two at a time, especially when entering the shedding cycle. Most of these snakes require a fairly high relative humidity in their cage to shed properly. An alternative to this can be provided by supplying a covered plastic shoebox of barely dampened, unmilled sphagnum moss in which they may hide and keep their skin soft and pliable.

**Subspecies:** As mentioned earlier, there are simply too many subspecies of milksnake to discuss individually. However, we will discuss two popular races found in the United States.

The **Scarlet kingsnake**, *L. t. elapsoides*, is a subspecies of southeastern United States and considered a coral snake mimic.

**Coloration:** In the United States, it is easy to differentiate between the scarlet kingsnake and the coral snake. The coral snake has the two caution colors, red and yellow, abutting one another. The scarlet kingsnake has the two caution colors separated by a band of black.

*Two color phases of the Mexican kingsnake, Lampropeltis mexicana, are shown here. Whether these are subspecies or color variants is arguable.*

The eastern coral snake also has a black nose, whereas the scarlet king is mainly red.

The scarlet kingsnake is easily recognized due to its red snout, narrow, supple torso, and 12–22 red bands. Neither the red nor the yellow (or white) scales have black tipping. It is usually active at night or at dusk on overcast,

rainy evenings. This snake averages 20 inches (51 cm) in total length. In the wild, they consume lizards and smaller snakes and also newly born mice. As captives, many wild-collected specimens retain their preference for lizard prey, particularly small skinks. Captive hatchlings that refuse other prey may accept baby skinks or tail sections from larger skinks.

The **Mexican milksnake** (*L. t. annulata*) is larger. As an adult, it is about 30 inches (76 cm) in total length, but may occasionally exceed a rather heavy-bodied 40 inches (102 cm). Its larger size allows a greater diversity of diet. Adults readily consume lizards, other snakes, and rodents. The neonates, 8–9 inches (20–23 cm) at hatching, can consume pinky mice.

Vividly ringed in red, black, and yellow (or white) but having a predominantly black belly and usually a black nose, they are found from central Texas southward into eastern Mexico.

*Gray-banded kingsnakes can be difficult to get to feed. Captive-born snakes are much easier to work with.*

## Gray-banded Kingsnake
### L. alterna

The gray-banded kingsnake is considered a prize species by many milksnake and kingsnake collectors. A moderate-sized species, adults attain a total length of about four feet (1.2 m).

**Coloration:** This species is the most variably colored of the kingsnakes found in the U.S., with color extremes so distinctly different that it was long thought to be two full species. One phase, initially called the Davis Mountain kingsnake, was described in 1901 as *L. alterna*. The second phase was first described in 1950 as a separate (and very rare) species, the Blair's kingsnake (*L. blairi*). When, in 1970, it was found that both *alterna* and *blairi* can hatch from a single clutch of eggs, the name *L. blairi* became invalid.

The "alterna phase" derives its name from the white-edged, dark bands that encircle the snake's olive-gray to gray body. Along the torso, these alternate—one is entire and the next is broken. The neck and tail are often patterned with blotches rather than bands. Red or orange may be present in the center of the complete bands on the neck or tail.

The "Blair's phase" of the gray-banded kingsnake is most variable, with some specimens very brilliantly colored, their white-edged black saddles containing broad areas of brilliant red or orange. Others may be very dark and become even darker with age, the red difficult to discern on older specimens.

Either phase may predominate in any given section of the species range. Within the U.S., the gray-banded kingsnake occurs in southwest Texas, with specimens found in immediately adjacent Eddy County, New Mexico, and also well southward in north central Mexico.

Reptile breeders across the country now offer hatchlings every year. Prices vary according to attractiveness, with the most brilliant or "classic" specimens being the most expensive. All tame and feed readily.

In nature, gray-banded kingsnakes prey primarily on lizards. Hatchlings are especially dependent on lizards. Even some captive-born baby specimens prefer lizards to mice.

## Sonoran Mountain Kingsnake
### *L. pyromelana* ssp.

Most people who are lucky enough to see this beautiful tri-colored snake in the wild are impressed at how cryptic the bright bands of red, black, and white are in nature.

They are found in high elevations of 3,000–9,000 feet (914–2,743 m) in pine, fir, and oak forests. Juniper and chaparral and numerous herbs form a sparse to heavy undercover.

The five subspecies, some of which are questionable, are defined by their markings (ring and scale counts) and by their site of origin. The expanses of desert lowland between the mountain ranges prevent crossover of specimens and ensure the integrity of the races.

Sonoran Mountain kingsnakes are much in demand by hobbyists because they are remarkably beautiful creatures that retain their brilliance and contrast throughout their life. All are clad in rings of brilliant red, jet black, and white. The only of the four subspecies that is not found in the United States is *L. p. knoblochi*, the beautiful Chihuahua Mountain king.

Sonoran Mountain kingsnakes are easily maintained, but require brumation (hiberna-

tion) to breed successfully. If merely kept as a pet, winter cooling is not required.

**Caution:** Wild kingsnakes (of all kinds) that prey heavily on amphibians are likely to have many endoparasites. Wild-collected kingsnakes should be watched carefully for signs of parasitism. Your veterinarian can use a stool sample to diagnose whether a problem exists.

# Bullsnakes, Gopher Snakes, and Pine Snakes
## Genus *Pituophis*

Despite their different appearances and belonging to different genera, the big constricting snakes of *Pituophis* are very closely allied to both the kingsnake and the rat snake. Occasional hybrids between gopher and rat snakes have been found in the wild, and hobbyists have produced similar hybrids.

*Pituophis* are heavy-bodied and small-headed. All are capable of powerful constriction, but may simply swallow small prey items alive. A projection on the glottis lets the bull, pine, and gopher snakes hiss loudly. The scales are prominently keeled. Aggressive at first, they can be tamed with handling.

All members of the genus *Pituophis* have an enlarged rostral (nose tip) scale to assist in burrowing, a habit best displayed by the very secretive eastern pine snakes.

**Habitats:** Preferences are for arid and semi-arid areas, plains, prairies, and sandhills. In the southeast where rain is plentiful, pine snakes are found in areas of sharp moisture runoff and well-drained soils.

**Habits:** Principally diurnal during periods of moderate temperature, these snakes may also be active at night during hot weather, especially bull and gopher snakes.

Although large specimens of the gopher, bull, and pine snakes that are accustomed to wild prey may be reluctant to accept laboratory mice and rats, this reluctance is seldom seen in hatchlings taken from the wild. The babies usually prove voracious feeders and fast growers. These snakes are all large as hatchlings, and most can easily accept a somewhat less than half-grown mouse.

When encountered in the field, *Pituophis* can prove nervous and irritable. Many will vibrate their tail strenuously and, if the snake is amid dead vegetation, the noise sounds like the "whirr" of a rattlesnake. The gopher, bull, and pine snakes are also top contenders with the wolf for championship in the "Three Little Pigs" contest—these snakes "huff and puff" (the noise sounds like a steam leak!), loop into a striking "S," and do everything possible to appear formidable. We would be very reluctant to reach for an irritated six-foot (1.8 m) pine snake. These snakes are not all bluff.

Although all are capable of burrowing, the pine snakes do so extensively.

Baby *Pituophis* tame quickly, but repeated and gentle handling will tame even wild adults.

*The bullsnake,* **Pituophis catenifer sayi,** *is the largest subspecies of gopher snake.*

However, be aware for the day your snake hisses and coils when you approach its cage. Gently lifting your snake first on a snakehook, then transferring it to your hand will often quiet it.

## Bullsnake
### *P. catenifer sayi*

**Coloration:** Like many in this genus, the dorsal blotches of the bullsnake are usually darker anteriorly and posteriorly than at mid-body. Blotch count is usually 41 or more. The blotches on the tail appear more like rings than saddles. The ground color of the bullsnake may vary according to the substrate on which it is found but is often a warm yellow or yellow-tan at midbody. In the last few years, several color morphs have been developed. Among these are chalk white (axanthic), with incomplete or obscured charcoal dorsal markings, albinos, snow, ghost, and hypomelanistic phases.

**Size:** With a record size of eight feet, four inches (2.54 m), the bullsnake is one of the largest snakes in North America. The adults are of impressively heavy girth.

**Range:** The bullsnake is the easternmost representative of this species. It ranges widely throughout the North American plains states, from southern Alberta, Canada, to well south of the U.S. border in northeastern Mexico.

Until recently, the bullsnake and the more westerly gopher snakes were considered sub-species of the pine snake, *P. melanoleucus.*

**Additional subspecies:** There are approximately 10 additional races of gopher snake, *P. catenifer* ssp., widely distributed over much of western North America from southern British Columbia and Saskatchewan southward to central mainland Mexico, all of the Baja Peninsula, and many of the islands. Of the various gopher

snakes, six are now commonly represented in herpetocultural projects: the Great Basin, the Pacific, the Sonoran, the San Diegan, the Central Baja, and the Cape gopher snakes. These six are all mainland and Baja forms and are being captive bred in fair numbers. A recent addition to the "captive breeding" list is the small Santa Cruz gopher snake.

The **Great Basin gopher snake** (*P. c. deserticola*) is the northernmost and one of the darker subspecies of gopher snakes. The dorsal blotches of this inland race are black and often interconnect with the lateral blotches. Although snakes of six feet (1.8 m) in length have been reported, 4.5–5 feet (1.4–1.5 m) in length is normal. The range includes southcentral British Columbia (Canada) southward to southeastern California, northern Arizona, and extreme northwestern New Mexico.

The **Pacific gopher snake** (*P. c. catenifer*) is perhaps the most variable and occurs naturally in both blotched and striped morphs. Albino specimens of both have been found. Availability and colorations of albinos have been artificially enhanced by captive-breeding projects. Hatchlings are *much* paler than the adults. This snake is usually seen in adult lengths of 4.5–5 feet (1.4–1.5 m). Its range includes much of western Oregon and California.

The **San Diegan gopher snake** (*P. c. annectens*) occasionally exceeds six feet (1.8 m) in length, but is more commonly four to five feet (1.2-1.5 m). This race also has an albino form, but most now available are the result of a long-ago intergrading with an albino Pacific. Range is from central California (Santa Barbara county) southward to central Baja California Norte. Although this snake seems most common in coastal areas, it is commonly found in mountains and desert regions.

The **Sonoran gopher snake** (*P. c. affinis*) is one of the most attractive and most commonly seen of the gopher snakes. The naturally occurring albinos have strawberry red saddles on a pearl white to pale pinky-white ground color. Commonly seen from southern Colorado southward through most of Arizona, New Mexico, and western Texas, its range continues well southward onto the Mexican mainland. Most adults are 4.5–5 feet (1.4–4.5 m).

The range of the **central Baja gopher snake** (*P. c. bimaris*) is in its name. Adult size is 4.5 to (rarely) six feet. Albinos and other color morphs have now been developed.

When adult, the **Santa Cruz Island gopher snake** (*P. c. pumilus*), also known as the **Channel Islands gopher snake**, is rarely longer than 36 inches (91 cm) and often smaller. At this length, it is the smallest member of the genus. Hatchlings are actually tiny, ranging from 6½ to 8 inches (17–20 cm) long.

Besides Santa Cruz Island, this snake is known to occur on one other Channel Island

and possibly on a third. Within its small natural range, this taxon is now largely protected. Fortunately, breeding programs are in place and Santa Cruz gopher snakes are now available.

Very few species in this genus are noted for brilliance of color (a few of the Mexican species have some peach or orange coloration), and the Santa Cruz Island gopher snake is one of the least colorful. The ground color is tan to pale straw yellow and the dorsal and lateral saddles and blotches (discrete posteriorly and coalescing anteriorly) are black.

We have not found these snakes to strike, bite, or even to hiss loudly (as many of their congenerics do), but they do squirm animatedly when handled.

Its small size makes it ideal for many hobbyists. It can be housed in a terrarium much smaller than must be provided for other gopher, bull, or pine snakes, and the prey items are correspondingly smaller as well.

The **Cape gopher snake** (*P. c. vertebralis*) ranges from La Paz, Baja California Sur, southward to the tip of the peninsula. This is the most brilliantly colored of the gopher snakes. The ground color is tannish-orange to buff anteriolaterally, lighter yellow posteriolaterally, rich orange on the anterior dorsum, and somewhat lighter posteriorly. The head is often a rich, unmarked orange on the crown, fading to light tan on the chin. This is one of the most coveted gopher snakes, and hatchlings command high prices. As common for this genus,

*The Pacific gopher snake, Pituophis c. catenifer, occurs in both the common blotched form as well as the more uncommon striped form. A striped albino is pictured.*

hatchlings and juveniles are paler than adults. The pallid coloration of a newly hatched specimen often gives little indication of the color and beauty it will one day have. Albino and "patternless" Cape gopher snakes have now been developed. Adult size is four feet (1.2 m), but some reach 5.5 feet (1.7 m).

## Pine Snakes
### P. melanoleucus ssp.

The four races of pine snake vary widely in color by subspecies, but to a lesser degree within a subspecies. As with the bull and gopher snakes, herpetoculturists have increased this variation by developing or enhancing both ground color and pattern intensity.

The **northern pine snake** (*P. m. melanoleucus*) is impressively large and often just as impressively belligerent. It has a curiously disjunct distribution from the Pine Barrens of New Jersey to central Kentucky in the north to central South Carolina and southern Alabama in the south, but is found only in a few tiny pockets of habitat.

This race, perhaps more than any other, is what hobbyists think of when pine snake is mentioned. Northern pines have long been coveted for their highly contrasting pattern. The ground coloration of most is chalk white, though buffs and reds may be seen. Selective breeding by herpetocuturists has created "red phase northern pines." The greatest authenticated length for this race is 83 inches (211 cm).

**Louisiana pine snake** (*P. m. ruthveni*) is the only pine snake found west of the Mississippi River. The most uncommon and poorly known of the pine snakes, it is found primarily in central western Louisiana and adjacent eastern central Texas, but at no point is its known

*Although not brightly colored, the Santa Cruz Island (Channel Island) gopher snake,* **Pituophis catenifer pumilus,** *is the smallest of the genus. It is now available to hobbyists in limited numbers.*

range contiguous with that of the bullsnake. This resident of pine flatwoods and dunes is marginally the smallest of the pine snakes, with the known record size being just 70.25 inches (178 cm).

Only recently have they become available to private herpetoculturists. Captive-breeding programs are making this snake more readily available, but it is still more expensive than most. Because of its comparative rarity, there is little effort by herpetoculturists to breed for albinism or other anomalies.

Until recently, the **black pine snake** (*P. m. lodingi*) was considered an expensive rarity by herpetoculturists. The success of captive-breeding programs has changed this, and it is now available to anyone who wants one.

Like many other dark snakes (kingsnakes and rat snakes), the degree of patterning visible on

*Occasionally, naturally occurring intergrades are found. This is an intergrade between the black pine and the Florida pine snake, Pituophis m. lodingi x P. m. mugitus.*

black pine snakes varies. Hatchlings tend to show more patterning than adults. Black pine snakes have been seen rarely in Washington Parish, Louisiana, and Escambia County, Florida.

It is perhaps because they are colored so very differently from the other subspecies of pine snakes that black pines are eagerly sought by hobbyists and breeders. The darkest snakes are the most in demand. Of all the many sub-species in this genus, the black pine is the only race to be so heavily pigmented with melanin.

Like other pine snakes, black pines reach 76 inches (193 cm) in length and are affiliated with sandy pineland habitats.

The **Florida pine snake** (*P. m. mugitus*) might be more appropriately called the "south-eastern" pine snake; its range includes eastern Georgia, southeastern South Carolina, and all but southernmost Florida. The ground color of hatchlings may be suffused with pink, peach, or pale-orange. Albinos and other color phases of this race have been developed. Although they seem more secretive than rare, the Florida pine snake is a regulated species in Florida. With a confirmed record length of 90 inches (228.6 cm), this is the largest pine snake.

## Mexican Bullsnake
### *P. deppei* ssp.

Once uncommon in herpetoculture, breeding programs are making the Mexican bullsnake a readily available snake. As with all snakes with which demand exceeds supply, the price of Mexican bullsnakes remains rather high. *P. d. deppei*, the more westerly race, is a snake of the Sierran elevations in central northern Mexico. It is the more prominently blotched of the two races, having rather precisely outlined charcoal to chocolate dorsal blotches against a ground color that may vary from gold to orange. Hatchlings are less brilliantly colored.

The more easterly race (*P. d. janni*) is found in the Mexican states of Coahuila, Nuevo Leon, Hidalgo, and Tamaulipas. It is pallid as a juvenile, with even the better defined ante-rior blotches appearing faded. The sandy tan ground color of the juveniles (which may have an orangish wash) intensifies with age. The ground color of the adult is golden to a rather

*The Florida pine snake, Pituophis melanoleucus mugitus, is the palest of the pine snake group.*

bright orange and is most intense at midbody. With age, the dorsal blotches *may* become better defined. Both races are known to exceed 5.5 feet (1.7 m) in total length.

**Caging:** Although young gopher snakes, bullsnakes, and pine snakes can be kept in plastic breeding trays, the large adults need sizable cages. We believe that a pair makes an ideal display when kept in a 75-gallon (284 L) (or larger) naturalistic terrarium.

**Breeding:** These snakes are now regularly bred in captivity. The methods for cycling the pine, bull, and gopher snakes reproductively are similar to those used to cycle rat and kingsnakes.

Although the clutches are relatively small, the eggs and hatchlings of all of these snakes are large. Hatchlings of the Great Basin gopher snake may be 12–14 inches (30–36 cm) in total length and those of the bull and Sonoran gopher snake may near 19 inches (48 cm) in length. In captivity, the largest clutches, largest eggs, and healthiest babies are obtained from the best-fed and healthiest females.

Incubation techniques for the eggs of these snakes is similar to that used for the eggs of the king and rat snakes.

# A Few Old World Rat Snakes

Thought to be more delicate and thus more "difficult" than their U.S. relatives, a few Old World rat snakes are now becoming popular in the U.S. Wild-collected Old World rat snakes **can** be more nervous and harder to handle than captive-bred specimens, and they should be examined for endoparasites as soon as possible; parasitic infections that were once

*The Mexican bullsnake's bright colors help make it a popular snake.*

considered life-threatening to snakes are now easily treated. Most Old World rat snakes are also relatively slow to attain maturity. From hatchling size, it may take three years for many to reach sexual maturity.

Although as effective constrictors as their U.S. counterparts, many immobilize a prey item by grasping it in their mouth and then throwing a single loop of their body over it.

## Radiated (or Copperhead) Rat Snake
*Caelognathus radiata*

**Coloration:** Unlike many of its Asian congenerics, the radiated rat snake is striped *anteriorly*, rather than posteriorly. The four stripes—two heavy dorsolateral stripes and two much thinner lateral stripes—are best defined on the anterior trunk. The ground color of *C. radiata* may vary from buff, tan, light brown or coppery-russet, to yellowish or greenish. The three dark stripes radiating from the eye and the dark collar (with which the uppermost of the orbital stripes connects) are representative of the species. Hypomelanistic (lacking much

*The radiated rat snake,* Coelognathus radiata, *is a pretty but defensive Asian species.*

melanin), anerythristic (lacking all red pigment), and albino specimens are also available.

**Behavior:** Wild-caught adults are very defensive. Even when vaguely threatened, the radiated esses its neck, inflates its throat, and vigorously strikes to defend itself. Because adults can grow to more than six feet (1.8 m) in length, the striking range is extensive. However, this snake would rather flee than fight. If neither fleeing nor aggressive behavior work, a frightened radiated rat snake may play dead, writhing, rolling over, and partially opening the mouth and extending the tongue. It

may then remain immobile for several minutes. They tame with handling.

**Range:** The radiated rat snake is found over a vast section of southeast Asia.

**Breeding:** Only recently have these been captive bred in the U.S. Until then, *all* available specimens were wild-collected imports. They do not seem to require even a period of cooling to cycle reproductively. However, a natural photoperiod does seem to help. Egg clutches of *C. radiata* consist usually of three to nine eggs, but sometimes more than 20 are laid by large, healthy females. Females are known to have several clutches during a single season. The hatchlings are usually 10 inches (25 cm) in total length.

**Diet:** Some wild-collected *C. radiata* can be problematic feeders. Housing them in sizable, quiet terraria with ample hiding areas may help. Offer a variety of prey items, including a small rat, a large mouse, a small hamster or gerbil, or a baby chick or quail. Captive-bred radiated rat snakes and even wild-collected babies will usually readily accept mice.

## Russian and Korean Rat Snakes
*Elaphe schrencki* and *E. anomala*

Although still considered "first cousins," the Russian and Korean rat snakes are no longer considered subspecies of *E. schrencki.* Instead, despite their external and physiological similarities and the ability of both to interbreed and produce sexually viable young, they are each considered a full species. The Russian rat snake (also called the Amur rat snake) has remained

Elaphe (Rhadinophis) prasina *is a beautiful, small, leaf green serpent that is now becoming popular with hobbyists.*

*Brown and silver when hatched, the Russian rat snake, becomes black and silver or black and yellow as an adult.*

E. schrencki and the Korean rat snake is now *E. anomala* (no longer *E. schrencki anomala*).

Both are large, very hardy species. These powerful constrictors can eat small rats when adult, but fare just as well on large mice. They often attain an adult length of five feet (1.5 m) and occasionally exceed six feet (1.8 m) by from one to a few inches. They are of moderately heavy girth. The 10-to-12-inch (25–30cm) long hatchlings are slender and often feisty, but the adults are usually quiet and, if slowly approached and gently handled, seldom strike or bite.

As hatchling, both species look similar, but the Korean form is often lighter in color and more irregular of pattern that the Russian. Adults are easily differentiated.

**Coloration:** Hatchlings of both species have a ground color of silvery tan to olive-tan. Hatchlings of the Korean rat snake are often three shades of gray: the light gray ground color and irregular darker gray bands (or saddles) that are narrowly edged with an even darker gray. More uncommonly, the hatchlings may have a tan ground color and display light-centered darker brown banding that is darkest on the outer edges. The Russian rat snake tends to have rather regular dark banding that is narrowly edged with very dark brown or black against a silvery tan ground color.

When adult, the banding of the Korean rat snake is less contrasting and the snake may be suffused with silvery gray or yellowish-tan. The adult Russian rat snake is much darker than it. The silvery ground color may remain but is often suffused with olive or some shade of yellow. The bandings are wide and normally jet black, but a brown phase is known.

**Breeding:** These snakes almost always require a 90-day period of winter cooling to breed successfully. A clutch may contain from five to 15 large eggs. At an incubation temperature of 80°–83°F (27–28°C) incubation takes from 45 to 55 days. The hatchlings usually feed readily on pinky mice.

**Range:** *Elaphe schrencki* is found in Siberia and Manchuria. *Elaphe anomala* is found in northeastern Korea.

## Leopard Snake
### Zamenis situla

**Coloration:** The leopard snake is one of the most beautiful members of the entire genus. It vaguely resembles the corn snake, but the two are *very* different. The "saddles" of the leopard rat snake are actually two rows of dark-edged strawberry dorsolateral spots, some of which may, or may not, be connected vertebrally by dorsal extensions. The ground color may be gray, olive-gray, tan, or pale olive-green. The head pattern is rather complex. A dark bar extends across the top of the head immediately anterior to the eyes. The top of the head is patterned with a black-outlined red blotch extending anteriorly from the forked neck blotch to a point just posterior to the eyes. A diagonal black temporal stripe is present on both sides.

**Size:** The leopard rat snake is the smallest of the European rat snakes. An average size for adults is between 26 and 30 inches (66–76 cm).

**Range and habitat:** This species ranges from eastern Turkey westward to Yugoslavia, and to eastern and southern Italy and Sicily. A disjunct population occurs in Ukraine, on the Crimean Peninsula. *Z. situla* is associated with hot, dry, often sandy, rocky, or sparsely wooded habitats. Like its European congeners, it prefers fencerows, ruins, and old stone walls.

**Diet:** Like many of the small and slender rat snakes of the world, it prefers small meals of nestling rodents and ground dwelling birds. Hatchlings and juveniles may feed on lizards and tree frogs. Our specimens had endoparasites and were also initially reluctant to feed on anything but wild mice (*Peromyscus*).

**Caging:** Our leopard rat snakes were housed in pairs or trios in a 20-gallon (76 L) terraria with a substrate of fallen leaves atop 1–2 inches (3–5 cm) of sandy soil and several secure hiding places. These are calm snakes that do not often bite. The temperature varies, but during the summer it is usually between 82° and 88°F (28–31°C) by day on the illuminated end and several degrees cooler on the dark end. Night temperatures are allowed to decrease by several degrees. Winter temperatures on the cool end of the terrarium by day are in the mid-60s°F (15.7°–18°C) to very low 70s (21–24°C). After the basking light is turned off in the late afternoon, the entire tank cools. We had been cautioned that preparing a suitable hibernaculum for these snakes would be difficult; this did not prove true. They survived the winter well under standard conditions, roused at two-week intervals for a lengthy drink.

**Breeding:** We have had several pairs of second-generation captive-bred leopard rat snakes breed successfully without having undergone hibernation. These individuals have experienced winter cooling as well as a natural photoperiod throughout the year. The clutches produced are small—only two to eight eggs. Incubation takes 60 days at 77°–82°F (25–28°C). Hatchlings measure close to one foot (31 cm) in length and will generally feed on mice soon after the postnatal shed.

**Subspecies:** None currently recognized.

**Comments:** Leopard rat snakes are coveted by collectors for their great beauty and comparative rarity. Expensive even in Europe, the few sold in the U.S. may be very expensive. Yet, they are of immense interest and well worth the specialized care they require.

*In coloration, the leopard rat snake, Zamenis situla, of Europe is quite like the corn snake of the United States.*

## Beauty Snakes
### *Orthriophis taeniura*

**Coloration:** The several poorly differentiated blotched races of this species are often referred to as beauty snakes. This is often prefixed with an origin such as "Taiwan," "Chinese," or "Yunnan." The rarely seen striped subspecies are often called cave rat snakes. Subspecies can be difficult to identify positively.

Only three of the blotched races are seen with any regularity in the U.S. pet trade. Color and pattern vary on all:

**1.** The Taiwan striped-tailed rat snake (*O. t. friesei*) seems to differ only in the *average* number of ventral scales (243–262).

**2.** The Chinese striped-tailed rat snake (*O. t. taeniura*) occurs on the Chinese mainland, Burma, and Thailand. The number of ventral scales on this race varies from 225–255.

**3.** The Yunnan striped-tailed rat snake (*O. t. yunnanensis*) (=*vaillanti*) is a (usually) more pallid and poorly patterned subspecies. It occurs in Yunnan Province, China.

The many races of *O. taeniura* vary greatly in appearance. Some (*taeniurus* and *friesei*) are proportionately heavy-bodied, strongly blotched anteriorly, striped posteriorly, and have a ground color of olive-buff to olive-yellow-green. *O. t. yunnanensis* (=*vaillanti*) is intermediate in appearance between the heavy, blotched forms and the attenuate racer-like subspecies. *O. t. vaillanti* tends to have less well-defined, double anterior body blotches or, if single, the blotches are usually narrow vertebrally.

*Although present in the hobby for years, the blue beauty snake,* **Othriophis taeniura** *ssp. from Vietnam, has not yet received a subspecific designation. The gaped mouth is a warning—but this snake rarely bites.*

*The very slender Tiawan beauty snake,* **Othriophis taeniura friesi,** *may attain a length of 8 feet (2.5 m).*

**Range:** The three subspecies above are only found in China. Other subspecies range southward from northern China throughout most of southeast Asia to Sumatra. They may be found from sea level to near 11,000 feet (3,353 m).

**Breeding:** All three are now being bred in the U.S. Some breeders use 90 days of hibernation; others use just a cooling period.

Females lay up to 14 (usually 6–10) eggs per clutch. At 80°F (27°C), incubation lasts for about 60 days. Hatchlings are very large, often being more than 16 inches (41 cm) in total length. They feed on furred baby mice.

**Size:** All races may attain a length of more than six feet (1.8 m). The published record size for *O. t. friesei* is 7 feet 9 inches (2.36 m), but more than 5.5 feet (1.7 m) is uncommon.

**Captive care:** Our *O. taeniura* specimens have seemed most content when kept cool. Terrarium temperature is usually 70°–76°F (21°–24°C). An illuminated basking area set at about 86°F (29°C) is provided. When keeping and breeding the various races, err toward coolness rather than heat. The snakes only sometimes avail themselves of the warmth of their hide box, especially if "traffic" is heavy near their cage.

All of the subspecies are nervous but easily kept and moderately difficult to breed.

# Garter, Ribbon, and Brown Snakes
## *Thamnophis* sp.

The garter and ribbon snakes are water-loving, small-bodied natricine snakes of North America. Garter snakes are generally heavier bodied and more terrestrial than the water-

loving ribbon snakes. The eastern forms of garter snakes seem to prefer worms, slugs, fish, frogs, and toads, whereas the western forms (and some eastern specimens) add nestling birds, rodents and other snakes and lizards to this diet. Among the favored foods of the ribbon snakes are fish and frogs; some will eat earthworms and slugs. Although most garter snakes are found close to water sources, some range long distances away from water.

**Breeding:** The American species are ovoviviparous, having large litters of live young. Annual cooling, if not actual extended hibernation, is needed for reproduction.

*The pattern and color of the eastern black-necked garter snake,* **Thamnophis cyrtopsis ocellatus,** *of Texas provides easy identification.*

**Comments:** Garter and ribbon snakes are active snakes and ready biters. Most are either diurnal or crepuscular, although some aridland forms may be nocturnal. Most thrive (but may not breed successfully) at room temperatures. However, if startled, even long-term captive garter snakes will dispel musk from cloacal glands. All have a rather high metabolism, and thus require frequent feeding that results, of course, in frequent stooling and frequent cage cleaning. Natricines will utilize a sizable water dish in which to submerge or fish. While doing the latter, they slide actively through the water, thoroughly dampening their cage. It is important that the cage dry quickly. Use a substrate that dries easily, is easily changed, and discarded.

*Many species of snakes, such as the eastern garter snake,* **Thamnophis s. sirtalis,** *display a wide range of color and pattern variations.*

## Common Garter Snake
### Thamnophis sirtalis

The common garter snake is widely distributed across North America. It may be found from the seaside dunes of the Atlantic Ocean to the seaside cliffs of the Pacific. It occurs from coast to coast in southern Canada and from the southernmost tip of the Florida Peninsula to just a few miles north of the United States/ Mexico border in California. It is absent, however, from the American southwest, northern Montana, southern Saskatchewan, and southern Alberta. Over most of those northern areas it is replaced by the Plains, *T. radix*, and wandering, *T. elegans*, garter snakes.

Certain races (and species) may be incredibly abundant in ideal habitats. The masses of breeding red-sided garter snakes (*T. s. parietalis*) documented by the National Geographic Society (and in other nature films) is one example.

**Coloration:** The eastern garter snake (*T. s. sirtalis*) is among the most variably colored of all the subspecies. A black(ish) snake boldly patterned with three longitudinal yellow stripes, the ground color may vary from olive through gray to tan, and the stripes from tan to bluish. In some populations the stripes are lacking (or poorly defined), and a checkerboard pattern is present. Melanistic specimens are commonly found in the Great Lakes region. Albino specimens are common, and at least one brightly colored orange specimen has been found in southeast North Carolina.

The Pacific Coast red-spotted garter snake, *T. s. concinnus*, is one of the most attractive species. It is found in northwest Oregon and extreme southwest Washington. Like many garter snakes it varies in coloration, but may combine ebony, vermilion and lemon in its pattern. The brilliant yellow vertebral stripe

*Captive-raised California red-sided garter snakes,* Thamnophis sirtalis infernalis, *are now available to hobbyists.*

is well defined; the lateral stripes are lacking. Some specimens are more subtly colored, lacking much or all of the red and having the lemon replaced by butter yellow.

The **San Francisco garter snake** (*T. s. tetrataenia*) is typified by a solid fire-orange to red-orange dorsolateral stripe along each side. An endangered subspecies now found only in a tiny portion of the remaining marshy habitat on the western San Francisco peninsula of central California, this specimen is one of the world's most beautiful snakes. The penalties for harassing or collecting them are harsh.

## Checkered Garter Snake
### T. marcianus marcianus

Named for its checkerboard pattern of black body spots, this snake of the southwestern United States and Mexico bears a downward projecting dark blotch on each side of its neck. The ground color is olive, and if present the light lateral stripes are pale and wavy.

In nature, they are most often found along water courses. During wet weather, it may wander far afield. Like other garter snakes, it feeds on amphibians, lizards, minnows, crustaceans, and baby rodents.

They thrive in captivity, requiring only a dry cage, a water source, and an ample diet. They have been bred extensively in captivity. Specimens from the lower Rio Grande Valley (and other perpetually warm areas) have cycled with only a slight winter cooling and a reduction in the photoperiod, but the best success has been achieved by hibernating them.

## Ribbon Snakes
### T. proximus ssp. and T. sauritus ssp.

There are only two species of ribbon snakes: the western (*T. proximus*) and the eastern (*T. sauritus*). Each has four subspecies.

**Care:** Despite their aquatic propensities, ribbon snakes do best in a primarily dry cage but do prefer a sizable water container in which they may fish and soak occasionally. They must

*Checkered garter snakes,* Thamnophis m. marcianus, *are available to hobbyists in both normal colors (seen here) and as albinos.*

be able to dry thoroughly between immersings to prevent the onset of skin disorders. Hiding places in the cage are an *absolute* necessity, due to their nervous nature. Security can be provided with live vining plants, plastic foliage, or dried grasses, combined with horizontal sticks and a small hide box.

**Range:** The western races are restricted to the central U.S., from Wisconsin to New Mexico to Texas to Louisiana, southward to Costa Rica. Collectively, the range of the eastern races embraces all of the eastern third of the U.S. and extreme southern Ontario, Canada.

**Appearance:** Both species share a similar appearance. On all ribbon snakes (with the sole possible exception being the Peninsula ribbon snake, *T. s. sackeni,* which may have the vertebral stripe reduced or absent), the stripes are precisely delineated. The eastern species has a dark ventrolateral stripe that involves the outermost tips of the ventral plates. Although present on the western species, the ventrolateral stripe is usually narrower, less well defined, and restricted to the body scales.

The western ribbon snake, *T. p. proximus,* is usually offered for sale. This attractive, graceful snake usually has yellowish side stripes and an orange vertebral stripe. Known to grow to more than 3 feet (.9 m) in total length, most adults are several inches shorter.

## Brown Snakes
*Storeria dekayi* ssp. and
## Red–Bellied Snakes
*S. occipitmaculata* ssp.

Although secretive, these are two of the most common "fencerow" and vacant lot snakes over much of eastern North America, found and collected from beneath bits of

*Gulf coast ribbon snakes,* **Thamnophis proximus orarius,** *often have an overall bluish sheen.*

ground debris. Although tiny (eight inches [20 cm] to 1 foot [31 cm] in length), these natricines can show as much spunk as their larger relatives. Their huffs, puffs, and feints are harmless bluff. They coil, inflate their body with air, flatten their head, and try to look as formidable as is possible for a snake less than a foot (31 cm) in length. Even a three-inch (8 cm) neonate will try this display.

*The several subspecies of brown snake can be difficult to identify. This is a Texas brown snake,* **Storeria dekayi texana.**

*Although the name is usually quite appropriate, some individuals of the northern red-bellied snake,* **Storeria o. occipitomaculata,** *may have yellow to gray bellies.*

In captivity, brown snakes will feed on worms; red-bellied snakes will feed on slugs.

# The "Odd-Toothed" Snakes

## Eastern Hog-Nosed Snake
### Heterodon platirhinos

The genus *Heterodon* contains three species. Although the western species eats a greater variety of food, all feed preferentially on toads. All three are characterized by upturned, enlarged rostral scales—a feature that gives them "hog" noses. The noses of both the southern and the western hognoses (*H. simus* and *H. nasicus*, respectively) are sharply upturned. The snout of the eastern hog-nosed snake, *H. platirhinos*, is the least accentuated.

Hog-nosed snakes are less feared than other snakes. Many people just seem to *like* them. Perhaps it is because they move more slowly than many other snakes, or maybe it is their inherent pudginess or repertoire of defensive ploys that endears them. Its defense strategies include striking at a tormentor with a closed mouth, spreading the head and neck in a fearsome "cobralike" display, and "playing possum."

Playing possum is usually the last defensive ploy. The threatened snake will suddenly writhe to and fro, mouth open, tongue lolling, as if in extreme agony. Suddenly it will roll over, belly up, then become quiet and limp—to all appearances, dead. It will show no signs of life unless turned rightside up. Then, quick as a wink, it will roll over again, as if the only way to impersonate a dead snake is to lie belly up.

**Caution:** Some people bitten by hog-nosed snakes experienced symptoms of mild envenomation. Localized mild to severe swelling and redness occurred. Although hog-nosed snakes seldom, if ever, purposely bite, care should be exercised when handling them. The toxic saliva is probably a mechanism for quickly disabling prey and does not seem to have been developed for defensive purposes.

**Coloration:** The eastern hog-nosed snake is a variably colored species. Examples vary from straw yellow between the dark dorsal blotches (darker laterally and brightest anteroverte-brally), to olive, to nearly jet black. Some areas have one phase or the other; other areas have all of the color schemes. Hatchlings are paler than adults. Albinos and hypomelanistic specimens have been found.

**Size:** Although lengths of more than 2.5 feet (76 cm) are seldom encountered, lengths of more than 3.5 feet (1.1 m) have been recorded.

**Range:** Eastern hog-nosed snakes range widely over most of the eastern half of the U.S. and in extreme southeastern Canada.

**Caging:** Because none are overly active, hog-nosed snakes seem content in fairly small cages. Many hobbyists keep them in plastic sweater boxes. Because we enjoy naturalistic terraria, we provide ours with a thick substrate of sand and place a clump or two of "bunch" or "field" grass in the cage. Its attractiveness, and the cover it provides the snakes, persist long after the grass has died. Rocks are also provided, as long as they can't settle on the snakes if they burrow beneath them. Fresh water is always available.

**Comments:** Hog-nosed snakes, collectively, are adept at burrowing and rooting out buried toads (a main component of their diets). In both pursuits, their keeled and upturned rostral scales serve them well. They are members of the grouping of colubrines known as xenodontines—the "odd-toothed" snakes. In the case of hog-noses, this refers to large teeth—the "toad stickers"—at the rear of the upper jaws. Toads, when confronted or grasped by a snake, inflate their bodies with air in an effort to make themselves unswallowable. This works with many snakes, but usually fails with hog-nosed snakes, which use their large teeth at the rear of the jaw to penetrate and deflate the toad's body.

**Should you feed it mice?** Some hobbyists and breeders advocate feeding mice to hog-nosed snakes. Although mice are a natural component of the diet of the western hog-nosed snake, they are less natural to either

*Because of its strange defensive antics (flattening of the neck and feigning of death), the eastern hog-nosed snake,* **Heterodon platirhinos,** *has long been a hobbyist favorite.*

the eastern or the southern species. All can be acclimated to take mice, initially by scenting a mouse with a toad. Some eastern and southern hog-nosed snakes may even accept mice voluntarily, but the long-term effects of such an unnatural diet have not yet been determined. Such a comparatively high-fat and difficult to digest prey item may affect lifespan and reproductive potential. Many hog-nosed snakes have died soon after eating live or freshly killed mice. Fewer deaths have been attributed to hog-nosed snakes that have ingested thawed, once-frozen mice. We believe that the feeding of mice to eastern and southern hog-nosed snakes should be approached with caution and the results monitored closely.

**Other species:** The southern and the western hog-nosed snakes are of quite similar appearance, the southern somewhat more brilliantly colored. The dark orbital bridle of the **southern hog-nosed snake** (*H. simus*) is usually not as well developed as on either the eastern or the western hog-nosed snake. The southern hog-nosed snake has about 25 dark dorsal blotches and often some pale orange or even peach coloring vertebrally. The colors tend to be brightest anteriorly. The sides are duskier.

The range of the southern hog-nosed snake includes a wide swath along the Atlantic Coastal Plain from central North Carolina to Gulf Coast central Mississippi (the Louisiana-Mississippi state line). As mentioned earlier, the southern hognose is also found southward in Florida to the region of Tampa Bay on Florida's west coast to Okeechobee County on the east..

The southern hog-nosed snake reaches a maximum of two feet (61 cm) in length.

Because toads are the favored food of the southern hog-nosed snake, few specimens have fed voluntarily on small pinkys.

The **western hog-nosed snake** (*H. nasicus*) has three similar-appearing subspecies: *H. n. gloydi*, the dusty hog-nosed snake of disjunct distribution along the extreme eastern part of the range (Texas, Oklahoma, Kansas), the Plains hog-nosed snake (*H. n. nasicus*) of the northern parts of the range (northern Texas and eastern New Mexico northward) and the Mexican hognose, *H. n. kennerlyi* (southern Texas southward). To identify the subspecies, we refer you to *Conant and Collins Field Guide to the Reptiles and Amphibians of the*

*Eastern and Central United States.* The range of the western hog-nosed snake (not differentiating for subspecies) extends southward through the Plains states from extreme southern Saskatchewan and southeastern Alberta Canada to far south into eastern Mexico.

They reach a length of just under 40 inches (1 m) and are the only species of hog-nosed snakes to routinely include rodents in their diet. Because of this, they are rapidly gaining the favor of herpetoculturists.

# Rough Green Snake
## *Opheodrys aestivus*

If you are squeamish about feeding traditional prey items to a snake but still have an interest in snakes, the insectivorous rough green snake is a species you should consider. Throughout its life it is an insectivore. In the wild it eats a variety of insects but particularly likes nonhairy caterpillars. In captivity it will eat vitamin-mineral dusted, gut-loaded crickets (crickets fed a vitamin and mineral enhanced diet before being offered as food), as well as other nonnoxious insects (see photo, page 4).

**Coloration:** This little snake is a rather standardized leaf-green dorsally, but may vary from white to butter yellow or yellowish-green ventrally. Hatchlings are much duller than the adults. The scales are keeled, hence the "rough."

**Size:** Some have measured more than 3.5 feet (1.1 m) in length, but the usual size is between two and three feet (61–91 cm).

**Range:** The rough (formerly, keeled) green snake may be found from southern New Jersey

*The southern hog-nosed snake, Heterodon simus, is the smallest species of this genus.*

*The brown house snake is a small snake that is being bred in an increasing array of colors.*

and eastern Kansas southward to the Gulf Coast. It is also found in northeastern Mexico.

**Breeding:** Southern specimens usually need only a slight winter cooling, lowered relative humidity, and lessened photoperiod to cycle. Examples from more northerly areas will require a 90-day period of full hibernation. Green snakes breed when the lengthening days of spring begin elevating temperatures and humidity increases. Healthy, well-acclimated rough green snakes may double clutch each year. The clutch size is quite small (1–10 eggs, often 3–6), and the eggs are noticeably elongate. Depending on temperature, humidity, and genetics, the incubation duration may vary from about four weeks to nine weeks or more. Hatchlings are a slender 7.5 inches (19 cm).

**Caging:** This snake does well in a terrarium setup and can co-exist with smaller cagemates, such as small frogs, salamanders, or lizards. This dainty and diminutive racer relative is persistently arboreal and very active in nature. We suggest captives be housed in a vertically oriented cage with growing, vining plants, such as philodendron or pothos, for the seclusion and security these little snakes seek and to help keep the cages humid. Rough green snakes will often not drink from a dish of standing water, preferring instead to drink droplets of misted water hanging from branches, leaves, terrarium sides, or from their own bodies. Many will use a water dish if the water is roiled with an aquarium air stone. We suggest a terrarium with a floor space of no less than 18 × 36 inches (46 × 91 cm) and prefer those with a

height of 30 or more inches (76+ cm). We also suggest that full-spectrum lighting and vitamin- and mineral-enhanced foods be provided. These little snakes will dehydrate quickly. A suitable regimen of providing water (probably misting) must be used daily.

Although most rough green snakes currently offered in the U.S. pet trade are wild collected, hobbyists are now beginning to breed them.

# Brown House Snake
## *Lamprophis fuliginosus*

Although the African genus *Lamprophis* contains several species, the only one to be firmly established in U.S. herpetoculture is *L. fuliginosus*, the brown house snake. It is small enough to be conveniently housed and is hardy.

**Coloration and appearance:** The brown house snake has a variety of pleasing natural colors—not all brown. Black specimens are found, as are olive ones. The colors most in demand in the U.S. are terracotta (called red by hobbyists) and golden brown. A pretty, warm chocolate phase is also favored. The venter may be pale yellow to opalescent. There are two narrow stripes on each side of the head. The upper one runs from the tip of the snout and extends back to the neck. The second stripe runs diagonally from the rear of the eye to the angle of the jaw. Amelanistic specimens are known. Its catlike eyes are large, and its head is

**Comments:** We believe brown house snakes are one of the best of the readily available pet trade species. As more colorful strains become steadily available, they should become more popular.

quite distinct from the neck. House snakes are crepuscular and nocturnal.

**Size:** As adults, brown house snakes can reach 2–3.5 feet (.61–1.1 m). Hatchlings measure between eight and 10 inches (20–25 cm) in length and usually accept pinky mice readily.

**Range:** It is a habitat generalist, especially prevalent in open grasslands. It is found near human dwellings (as indicated by its name) and throughout most of subsaharan Africa.

**Breeding:** The largest, healthiest females produce up to 15 eggs per clutch, and several clutches may be laid annually at 4–6-week intervals. To cycle, these fecund snakes require only a slight winter cooling. Although we maintained them with a natural photoperiod, this does not seem as important as with certain other snake species. Eggs incubate for about two months at 82°F (28°C).

**Caging:** Newly captured specimens are prone to bite. However, they acclimate and quiet rather quickly. These are not overly active snakes. A young pair can be easily maintained in a 15-gallon (57 L) terrarium. With a floor space of 12 × 24 inches (30 × 61 cm) and a height of 12 inches (30 cm). The cage should have several secure hiding areas, a small, untippable water dish, and an easily cleaned substrate. A summer temperature of 78°–86°F (26–30°C) seems acceptable. During the daytime, we provide a basking area of about 90°F (32°C). Only gravid females use this basking area with any regularity.

# Neotropical Indigo Snakes, the Cribos
## *Drymarchon corais* ssp.

Big, messy, often short-tempered, heavily parasitized, and only marginally pretty, many hobbyists still find cribos appealing. These are wide-ranging, very active habitat generalists related to the indigo snakes.

The **eastern indigo snake** (*D. c. couperi*) is a federally endangered species that can neither be collected nor sold in interstate commerce in the United States, even if legally held and bred, without an appropriate permit. There are numerous hobbyists breeding the race. Before being regulated, this snake was one of the most eagerly sought by reptile collectors.

Although the **Texas indigo** (*D. c. erebennus*) is not considered endangered, it is a protected species both in Texas and in Mexico. It cannot be legally collected without a permit.

The **yellow-tailed cribo,** *Drymarchon corais corais,* is the most brightly colored of these.

## Black-tailed cribo
### *D. c. melanurus*

**Coloration:** The amount of black coloration on the posterior of the black-tailed cribo varies greatly. Some may lack most of the black pigmentation; others may be black from tip of the tail to a point well anterior of midbody. In all cases, dark markings radiate downward from the eye to the lip, a vertical dark slash is at the rear of the jaw, and a heavy diagonal black slash is on each side of the neck.

The scales of the anterior of the body and head are olive-yellow to olive-tan. Healthy adults can be heavy bodied, but because of an almost invariable abundance of parasites, wild adults are very thin, with prominent backbones. Hatchlings look like diminutives of the adults, but are proportionately more slender.

**Size:** Although not the longest subspecies, it often exceeds seven feet (2.1 m) in length and may be as much as 10 feet (3 m).

**Range:** Found throughout much of Central America, it is an adept climber, fast on the ground, and capable of swimming if necessary. It is found in forest openings, natural savanna edges, and man-made clearings.

**Breeding:** Cribos and indigo snakes have moderate clutches of large eggs. Hatchlings vary between 16 and 24 inches (41–61 cm) in total length. At hatching, they are well able to eat small mice, frogs, and other small prey.

In keeping with their tropical habitat, these cribos can be cycled reproductively with just a moderate winter cooling combined with a lowered relative humidity and a reduced photoperiod. This cycling should last for 45–65 days. Cribos will often breed during, or even at the advent of, this period. This is in keeping with eastern indigos, which are such effective thermoregulators that they can keep active in all but the very coldest weather and breed during the winter months. Sperm may be held for several months prior to fertilizing the eggs.

They may lay at any time of the spring or early summer (no cribo/indigo has double clutched at our facility), and incubation can take from two to more than two and a half months.

It seems that cribos fed a varied diet of birds, mammals, and amphibians breed more readily than those fed only rodents.

**Caging:** Cribos are big snakes that in nature are active "search and overpower" predators.

As expected from such a snake, they do best in large cages. A cage with a floor space of

*A protected species, the eastern indigo snake,* **Drymarchon corais couperi,** *requires a permit prior to being sold or bartered in interstate commerce.*

4 × 8 feet (1.2 × 2.5 m) would probably suffice for a pair of cribos, but larger may be better. Although limbs or elevated platforms are not mandatory, the snakes will use them if provided. A large receptacle of fresh water is for both drinking and soaking. The water should be frequently cleaned and sterilized to help prevent transference of endoparasites. Wild-collected cribos should be checked for endoparasites as soon as possible.

Adults taken from the wild may strike savagely at movements outside of their cage causing nose injuries. It may be necessary to tape opaque paper or cloth to the front of the glass until the snakes become less agitated.

Although it takes a dedicated person to keep a cribo, with proper care, persistent gentle handling, and slow keeper movements, these snakes will usually quiet down and thrive.

# A FINAL WORD

*Once reviled, snakes are now the pets of choice in many households. They are clean and easily cared for pets.*

There has been such a proliferation of serpent-related knowledge in the last quarter century that the burgeoning hobby of today is barely recognizable as the hobby we remember from the 1970s (and before). Corn snakes, kingsnakes, gopher snakes, boas, and pythons—all are being captive-bred in such numbers that it now seems they come from a bottomless pit. For example, there is a "captive-bred expo" in Daytona, Florida, each August that brings together some 450 reptile vendors (mostly of snakes) and 10,000 hobbyists in four auditorium-sized conference rooms. We marvel at this and compare the days of our childhoods when we felt gratified if we could find just a single other enthusiast with whom to share our experiences.

The immense popularity of snakes as pets may have a downside. Collecting pressures on wild snake populations continue to increase each year. Additionally, thousands upon thou-

sands of snakes are killed on roadways and by humans who have not yet learned to appreciate these creatures of the wild. Increased predator populations (especially dogs, cats, raccoons, and in the southern tier states, the fire ants), take an unknown, but probably very significant toll. It is unlikely that snake populations in some areas can sustain such unnatural pressures and remain viable much longer. If we hope to preserve the wild populations of many snakes for our and our children's enjoyment, we, as naturalists and hobbyists, must begin thinking and obeying practices of conservation.

In this book, we have tried to offer you an overview of the snake species most favored by American hobbyists. Most are also of interest to hobbyists elsewhere in the world. We hope that our comments on these pages will help you develop a greater interest and better understanding of the varied animals integral to the enjoyment of our hobby and to the success of the business of herpetoculture as we know it today.

Dick and Patti Bartlett

*The insectivorous smooth green snake, Opheodrys vernalis, has proven a difficult captive.*

# INFORMATION

## Affinity Groups

Once obscure, herpetoculture is now a recognized hobby. In fact, many hobbyists are surprised to find how many others share their interests. Snake keepers, both casual and professional, outnumber the keepers of all other groups. Detailed additional information can be obtained from a fellow hobbyist or, in today's computer-oriented society, in any number of online services. You can find other enthusiasts through your local pet stores, libraries, universities, and community colleges.

Another source of information is herpetology groups. There are generalized groups of hobbyists in many large cities of the world, as well as professional societies such as the Society for the Study of Reptiles and Amphibians (SSAR).

## Herpetologically Oriented Ecotours

MT Amazon Expeditions
10821 SW 48 Terrace
Miami, FL 33165-6122
786-232-2674 (East Coast)
619-562-2422 (West Coast)
Amazon-Ecotours.com

## Helpful Reading
### Magazines (USA and England)

**Reptiles Magazine:** A magazine dedicated primarily to herpetoculture and conservation. *Reptiles* is a high-quality monthly publication. Subscription information may be obtained from *Reptiles Magazine*, P.O. Box 6050, Mission Viejo, CA 92690-6050.

**Herpetological Review** and the **Journal of Herpetology:** The Society for the Study of Reptiles and Amphibians is a professional-level organization that publishes a nontechnical

periodical, *Herp Review*, and a more scholarly journal, *Journal of Herpetology*. Subscriptions are available from SSAR, Department of Zoology, Miami University, Oxford, OH 45056.

**Copeia:** The American Society of Ichthyologists and Herpetologists publishes *Copeia*, a technical journal which includes reptiles, amphibians, and fish. Subscription information is available from ASIH Business Office, Dept. of Zoology, Southern Illinois University, Carbondale, IL 62901-6501.

**Herpetologica:** This quarterly is available through the Herpetologist's League, c/o Maureen A. Donnelly, College of Arts and Sciences, Florida International University, North Miami, FL 33181.

## Books

Arnold, E. N., and J. A. Burton. *A Field Guide to the Reptiles and Amphibians of Britain and Europe.* London: Collins, 1978.

Bartlett, Richard D. *In Search of Reptiles and Amphibians.* Leiden: E. J. Brill, 1988.

Bartlett, Richard D. *Digest for the Successful Terrarium.* Morris Plains, NJ: TetraPress, 1989.

Bartlett, Richard D. and Patricia P. Bartlett. *Corn Snakes and Other Rat Snakes: A Complete Pet Owner's Manual.* Hauppauge, NY: Barron's, 1996.

Bartlett, Patricia P., and Ernie Wagner. *Pythons: A Complete Pet Owners Manual.* Hauppauge, NY: Barron's, 1997.

Conant, Roger, and Joseph T. Collins. *A Field Guide to Reptiles and Amphibians; Eastern and Central North America.* Boston: Houghton Mifflin Co., 1991.

Dowling, Herndon G. "A taxonomic study of the rat snakes, genus *Elaphe Fitzinger*. Vol. II. The

*The Kenyan sand boa,* Gongylophis colubrinus loveridgei, *is very popular with hobbyists.*

subspecies of *Elaphe flavirufa* (*Copeia*)." Ann Arbor, MI: University of Michigan, 1952.

Dowling, Herndon G. "A taxonomic study of the rat snakes. Vol. VI. Validation of the genera *Gonyosoma Wagler* and *Elaphe Fitzinger* (*Copeia*)." Ann Arbor, MI: University of Michigan, 1958.

Markel, Ronald G., and R. D. Bartlett. *Kingsnakes and Milksnakes: A Complete Pet Owner's Manual.* Hauppauge, NY: Barron's, 1995.

Mehrtens, John M. *Living Snakes of the World in Color.* New York: Sterling Publishers, 1987.

Pope, Clifford H. *The Reptiles of China.* New York: American Museum of Natural History, 1935.

Smith, Malcolm A. *The Fauna of British India, Ceylon and Burma, Reptilia and Amphibia.* Vol. III Serpentes. London: Taylor and Francis, 1943.

Stebbins, Robert C. *A Field Guide to Western Reptiles and Amphibians.* Boston: Houghton Mifflin Co., 1985.

Staszko, Ray, and Jerry G. Walls. *Rat Snakes: A Hobbyist's Guide to Elaphe and Kin.* Neptune, NJ: TFH, 1994.

Wagner, Doug. *Boas: A Complete Pet Owner's Manual.* Hauppauge, NY: Barron's, 1996.

West, Larry, and William P. Leonard. *How to Photograph Reptiles and Amphibians.* Mechanicsburg, PA: Stackpole, 1997.

Wright, Albert H., and A. A. Wright. *Handbook of Snakes.* Vol. I. Ithaca, NY: Comstock, 1957.

**Important Note**

The subject of this book is the keeping and care of nonpoisonous snakes. Snake keepers should realize, however, that even the bite of a snake regarded as nonpoisonous can have harmful consequences—so see a doctor immediately after any snake bite.

Handling giant serpents requires a lot of experience and a great sense of responsibility. Carelessness can be deadly! Inexperienced snake keepers and snake keepers who have small children are therefore urgently advised not to keep giant serpents.

Electrical appliances used in the care of snakes must carry a valid "UL approved" marking. Everyone using such equipment should be aware of the dangers involved with it. It is strongly recommended that you purchase a device that will instantly shut off the electrical current in the event of a failure in the appliances or wiring. A circuit-protection device with a similar function has to be installed by a licensed electrician.

# GLOSSARY

**Aestivation:** A period of warm weather inactivity that is often triggered by excessive heat or drought.

**Albino:** Lacking black pigment.

**Ambient temperature:** The temperature of the surrounding environment.

**Anerythristic:** Lacking red pigment.

**Anterior:** Toward the front.

**Anus:** The external opening of the cloaca; the vent.

**Arboreal:** Tree dwelling.

**Boid/Boidae:** Boas and pythons.

**Brille:** The transparent "spectacle" covering the eyes of a snake.

**Brumation:** Often used to describe reptilian and amphibian hibernation.

**Caudal:** Pertaining to the tail.

**cb/cb:** Captive bred, captive born.

**cb/ch:** Captive bred, captive hatched.

**Cloaca:** The common chamber into which digestive, urinary, and reproductive systems empty and which itself opens exteriorly through the vent or anus.

**Colubrine/Colubridae:** The largest of the snake groupings, comprising such snakes as garters, rats, kings, and gophers.

**Congeneric:** In the same genus.

**Constricting:** To wrap tightly in coils and squeeze.

**Convergent evolution:** Evolution of two unrelated species as the result of environmental (or other) conditions.

**Crepuscular:** Active at dusk or dawn.

**Deposition:** The laying of the eggs or birthing of young.

**Deposition site:** The spot chosen by the female to lay her eggs or have her young.

**Dimorphic:** A difference in form, build, or coloration involving the same species; often sex-linked.

**Diurnal:** Active in the daytime.

**Dorsal:** Pertaining to the back; upper surface.

**Dorsolateral:** Pertaining to the upper sides.

**Ecological niche:** The precise habitat utilized by a species.

**Ectothermic:** Relying on external sourcecs for body temperature regulation.

**Endothermic:** Able to regulate body temperature internally.

**Erythristic:** A prevalence of red pigment.

**Form:** An identifiable species or subspecies.

**Fossorial:** Adapted for burrowing; a burrowing species.

**Genus:** A taxonomic classification of a group of species having similar characteristics. The genus is classified between the next higher designation of "family" and the next lower designation of "species." *Genera* is the plural of genus. It is always capitalized when written.

**Glottis:** The opening of the windpipe.

**Gravid:** The reptilian equivalent of mammalian pregnancy.

**Gular:** Pertaining to the throat.

**Heliothermic:** Pertaining to a species that basks in the sun to thermoregulate.

**Hemipenes:** The dual copulatory organs of male lizards andsnakes.

**Hemipenis:** The singular form of hemipenes.

**Herpetoculture:** The captive breeding of reptiles and amphibians.

**Herpetoculturist:** One who indulges in herpetoculture.

**Herpetologist:** One who indulges in herpetology.

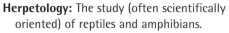

**Herpetology:** The study (often scientifically oriented) of reptiles and amphibians.

**Hibernacula:** Winter dens.

**Hybrid:** Offspring resulting from the breeding of two species.

**Hydrate:** To restore body moisture by drinking or absorption.

**Insular:** Island-dwelling.

**Intergrade:** Offspring resulting from the breeding of two subspecies.

**Jacobson's organs:** Highly enervated olfactory pits in the palate of snakes and lizards.

**Juvenile:** A young or immature specimen.

**Keel:** A ridge (along the center of a scale).

**Labial:** Pertaining to the lips.

**Lateral:** Pertaining to the side.

**Melanism:** A profusion of black pigment.

**Middorsal:** Pertaining to the middle of the back.

**Midventral:** Pertaining to the center of the belly or abdomen.

**Monotypic:** Containing but one type.

**Natricine/Natricinae:** A member of the subfamily containing garter water, brown, and other related colubrine snakes.

**Nocturnal:** Active at night.

**Ontogenetic:** Age-related (color) changes.

**Opisthoglyphous/opisthoglyph:** A colubrine snake with enlarged teeth in the rear of its upper jaw and a variably toxic saliva.

**Oviparous:** Reproducing by means of eggs that hatch after laying.

**Ovoviviparous:** Reproducing by means of shelled or membrane-contained eggs that hatch prior to or at deposition.

**Photoperiod:** The daily or seasonally variable length of the hours of daylight.

**Poikilothermic:** A species with no internal body temperature regulation. The old term was "cold-blooded."

**Postocular:** To the rear of the eye.

**Prey imprinting:** Preferring prey of only a particular species or color.

**Race:** A subspecies.

**Rostral:** The (often modified) scale on the tip of the snout.

**Rugose:** Not smooth. Wrinkled or tuberculate.

**Saxicolous:** Rock-dwelling.

**Scute:** Scale.

**Species:** A group of similar creatures that produce viable young when breeding. The taxonomic designation which falls beneath genus and above subspecies. Abbreviation: "sp."

**Subspecies:** The subdivision of a species. A race that may differ slightly in color, size, scalation, or other criteria. Abbreviation: "ssp."

**Sympatric:** Occurring together.

**Taxonomy:** The science of classification of living things.

**Terrestrial:** Land dwelling.

**Thermoreceptive:** Sensitive to heat.

**Thermoregulate:** To regulate (body) temperature by choosing a warmer or cooler environment.

**Thigmothermic:** Pertaining to a species (often nocturnal) which thermoregulates by being in contact with a preheated surface such as a boulder or tarred road surface.

**Vent:** The external opening of the cloaca; the anus.

**Venter:** The underside of a creature; the belly.

**Ventral:** Pertaining to the undersurface or belly.

**Ventrolateral:** Pertaining to the sides of the venter (belly).

# INDEX

## About the Author

R. D. Bartlett is a herpetologist and herpetoculturist who has authored more than 425 articles and three books and coauthored an additional 11 books. He lectures extensively and has participated in field studies across North and Latin America. Bartlett is a member of numerous herpetological and conservation organizations, a co host on an on-line reptile and amphibian forum, and a contributing editor of *Reptiles Magazine*.

Patricia Bartlett is a biologist and historian who has authored five and coauthored 11 books. A museum administrator for the last 15 years, she has worked in both history and science museums.

In 1970, the Bartletts began the Reptilian Breeding and Research Institute (RBRI), a private facility. Since its inception, more than 200 species of reptiles and amphibians have been bred at RBRI, some for the first time in the United States under captive conditions. Successes at the RBRI include several endangered species.

## Acknowledgments

To Rob MacInnes of Glade, Herp, Inc., Chris McQuade of Gulf Coast Reptiles, (Ft. Myers, FL), to Bill Love of Blue Chameleon Ventures (Alva, FL), Regis Opferman (Pueblo, CO), and Kenny Wray (Tallahassee, FL), we extend thanks for the photographic opportunities. Bill Griswold (Spring Hill, FL) and Billy Griswold, DVM (Priority Pets; Phoenix, AZ), unhesitatingly provided us with information regarding their breeding programs for hog-nosed snakes and rough green snakes. Bill Brant (The Gourmet Rodent of Gainesville, FL) afforded me the opportunity to photograph his brown house snakes, and Carl May shared with me some of his experiences with both brown house snakes and rainbow boas. John Decker provided more than marginal insight into his breeding programs with his favored rosy and Keys variant rat snakes.

A note of thanks is due Doug Wagner for his critical evaluation of—and pertinent contributions to—our manuscript as well as to our editor, Kristen Girardi, for guiding us along the intricate pathways leading to publication.

## Cover Photos

All cover photos courtesy of Richard D. Bartlett and Patricia P. Bartlett.

## Photo Credits

All interior photos courtesy of Richard D. Bartlett and Patricia P. Bartlett.

*All inquiries should be addressed to:*
Barron's Educational Series, Inc.
250 Wireless Boulevard
Hauppauge, NY 11788
**www.barronseduc.com**

*Library of Congress Catalog Card No. 2009045903*

ISBN-13: 978-0-7641-4343-4
ISBN-10: 0-7641-4343-3

**Library of Congress Cataloging-in-Publication Data**
Bartlett, Richard D., 1938-
  Snakes: a complete pet owner's manual / R. D. Bartlett and Patricia P. Bartlett.
    p. cm.
  Includes bibliographical references and index.
  ISBN-13: 978-0-7641-4343-4 (alk. paper)
  ISBN-10: 0-7641-4343-3 (alk. paper)
 1. Snakes as pets 2. Snakes I. Bartlett, Patricia Pope, 1949- II. Title.
SF459.S5B376 2010
639.3'96—dc22                    2009045903

Printed in China
9 8 7 6 5 4 3 2 1